IRON SHOES

C. Roy Angell

IRON SHOES

BROADMAN PRESS
Nashville, Tennessee

CONTENTS

Iron Shoes . . . 1

The Uncut Pages of Life . . . 9

Strange Harmonies . . . 19

The Lighter of Candles . . . 27

Life Is an Echo . . . 36

Diamond Dust . . . 44

The Overflow Ministry . . . 55

Rizpah . . . 64

Hinds' Feet . . . 75

Keeping Life's Windows Clean . . . 85

The Second Mile . . . 94

This Glorious Gospel . . . 106

IRON SHOES

1

Iron Shoes

Thy shoes shall be iron and brass.—
DEUTERONOMY 33:25.

The most beautiful cluster of promises in the Old Testament is found in one of the Bible's most unread books. In the thirty-third chapter of Deuteronomy three promises nestle together: "As thy days, so shall thy strength be"; "Underneath are the everlasting arms"; and "The eternal God will be thy refuge." But God never puts promises like these in a group without a reason, and that reason is stated in the preceding verse, "Thy shoes shall be iron and brass." God was lifting the veil of the future a little for some of his chosen people to see. He was saying to them, "Your road is going to be so rough that you will

---

NOTE: From *Best Sermons* (1947-48). Used by permission of the editor, Dr. G. Paul Butler.

need iron shoes." Then he added the assurance of these three beautiful promises.

As I read them today I do not think that they were confined to this tribe of Asher, but rather God was stating the facts about a normal life, for there comes a day in the life of most of us when God hands us a pair of iron shoes and it is of vital importance that we wear them as a Christian should. We can do this only if we have the faith to appropriate these three beautiful promises.

I saw this admirably done not so long ago. I had gone to a high school to preach the baccalaureate sermon. As the processional began, I was startled to see how slowly it moved, and I kept wondering about it until into the door at the end of the long aisle there came a wisp of a girl. She was walking with much difficulty; every step jarred her whole body. Then I realized that she was braced with iron from her head to her heels; and I realized another thing which gave me a thrill—the speed of the procession was timed to make it easy for her. Half way down the aisle her cap jarred down over her eyes. I saw her smilingly nudge the big two-hundred-pound boy who was marching with her. With an answering smile, he adjusted her cap, because her arms couldn't reach it.

When the time came, the principal conferred the honors, all but one, for, at the close of the presentations he said, "There is one other medal given by the students. It will be presented by the captain of the football team to a young lady who has been a great inspiration to our entire school."

The same big, two-hundred-pound boy came forward leading the little girl in the iron braces. His speech was

2

something like this: "This is the biggest medal I ever saw, because every one in the school wanted to have a part in buying it, but it isn't big enough to express our gratitude to this young lady. On one side of it is inscribed her name, Christine. On the other is our pet name for her, Miss Inspiration. Through these years of school life she has worn iron braces and suffered continually, but no hardship has ever been tough enough to wipe the smile off her face. Sometimes when the going has gotten rough for us out on the athletic field or elsewhere, someone invariably would mention her name and we just grin and buckle down."

When the commencement exercises were over and I finally got through the crowd to Miss Christine, I asked what appeared to her a superfluous question, for I asked if she were a Christian.

Astonishment was written all over her face, and her answer was a classic. "No one could be a tenth of what that boy, in his exaggeration, said about me and not be a Christian."

God does not ask us all literally to wear iron shoes like this little girl wears, but few of us ever walk long on life's roadway without finding a pair of iron shoes. God never promised a Christian that there would be no suffering. The grandest little man that ever lived, Paul, wore iron shoes from the beginning to the end of his ministry. One day when the load got too heavy, he asked God to take them away, but instead God gave him more grace. Even Christ, the only begotten Son of God, walked into the garden of Gethsemane, on down through Pilate's court, and up the hill of Golgotha wearing iron shoes.

Quo Vadis ends with a climactic picture of Simon Peter trying to run away because the iron shoes were hurting his feet, but when he met Christ going to take his place on the firing line he put them back on and went back to his martyrdom.

God knew if we Christians were going to wear iron shoes like real soldiers of the cross we would need these three beautiful promises to lean upon. There is no repetition here. Look closely at each one of them:

The first one is: "As thy days, so shall thy strength be." This was Alexander Maclaren's favorite text. He said he learned how true this verse was when he accepted his first job in Glasgow. He was just sixteen, and his home was about six miles from the big city. Between his home and Glasgow there was a deep ravine that was supposed to be haunted. Some really terrible things had happened in it and he was afraid to go through it even in the day time. At night it was out of the question.

On Monday morning his father walked with him to work and in parting said, "Alec, come home as fast as you can when you get off Saturday night."

Thinking of that deep ravine, Maclaren said he answered his father, "Father, I will be awfully tired Saturday night. I will come home early Sunday morning."

But his father was adamant, "No, Alec. You have never been away from home before, and these five days are going to seem like a year to me. Come home Saturday night."

Reluctantly Alec answered, "All right, Father, Saturday night." All the week long Alec said he worried about that black ravine. When Saturday night came, he was more scared than ever, but he wrapped up his belongings and went out to the end of the gulch. He said, "I whistled to keep my courage up, but when I looked down into that inky blackness I knew I couldn't go. The tears came unbidden, and then suddenly I heard footsteps in the ravine coming up the path. I started to run but hesitated, for those footsteps were very familiar.

"Up out of the darkness into the pale light, as I watched, came the head and shoulders of the grandest man on earth. He was bound to have known I was scared, but he only said, 'Alec, I wanted to see you so badly that I came to meet you.' So shoulder to shoulder we went down into the valley and I was not afraid of anything that walked."

How beautifully for every Christian this illustrates this most essential truth. "As thy days, so shall thy strength be." When the dark and unknown passages of life come, Christ also comes. Wasn't it Laurence Sterne, one of the first of the English novelists who wrote, "God tempers the wind to the shorn lamb"? Maybe this was the lesson that God was trying to teach us when he sent the manna to his children in the wilderness. There was just enough for each day.

The second promise, "Underneath are the everlasting arms," no doubt had its origin in something the writer of this book had often seen in the mountainous wilderness over which he had traveled. In the preceding chapter he refers to it. He had seen an eagle teaching its young to fly. The ceremony began with the destruction of the nest. The old eagle tore up the nest and threw the pieces

5

over the cliff. Then she took the little eaglet on her broad back and, circling, carried him high into the sun. Then she tilted her wings and slid him off into space.

Fluttering, screeching, screaming, he drifted down. The old eagle circled around him. Long before the eaglet reached the sharp crags and rocks below, she glided under him and caught him on her strong wings. Two or three times she repeated this as if to say, "See, you cannot fall for underneath are the everlasting wings." The writer changed the picture just a little and made it read that "underneath are the everlasting arms of God." We need this message badly, for we do not travel far along life's roadway until we realize we need God's help.

When David described God as "the Good Shepherd," he was using the most endearing and realistic words he could find—for the Good Shepherd would do as David had done, fight the beasts of the forest and the birds of the air for his flock. If one of the flock was wounded or sick, he found underneath him the everlasting arms, tender and strong, the arms of the Good Shepherd.

The next promise, "The eternal Lord is thy refuge," states in beautiful poetry another great promise that we will have to lean upon if we wear our iron shoes like a Christian should. We need to know that we have a sanctuary into which we can go—that our strength may be renewed like the eagle's. There are times when life is too much for us and we cannot keep our chins up. We are wounded and sick of heart. We need a refuge.

Maybe this is what Jesus was talking about when he said, "Go into thy closet and shut the door and stay alone with God." Certainly this is what Jesus did. He left his disciples and climbed up into the mountain and spent the night with his Father. As someone beautifully stated it, "He went into the silence with God."

One of the greatest sermons that Dr. George Mc-Daniel ever preached was not preached from the pulpit, but preached from the saddle one morning at dawn, and just to me. We had been enjoying for sometime the music of a pack of fine foxhounds as they chased a wily red fox. On this particular occasion we had ridden across ahead of the dogs to the high rock cliff in which this old red fox had taken refuge several times before. "Marse George," as we called him, was eager for a glimpse of the fox that his dogs couldn't catch. We had concealed our horses in the bushes and were sitting very silently and still when around the edge of the high cliff on a shelf of rock the big, red fox nonchalantly trotted to the mouth of the dark, deep den. He stopped a moment and lifted his head to listen. The dogs were a great distance away, so he casually sat down and began to smooth his fur and lick his paws. At intervals he would prick up his ears, listen intently, and then relax. Finally, when the dogs got close, he trotted unhurriedly into the dark cavern behind him and, I can imagine, sat relaxed and unafraid as he listened to the furor of the hounds as they surrounded the entrance to his home.

Dr. McDaniel laid his hand over on the pommel of my saddle and with deep emotion said, "Roy, there's a great sermon. When you have a safe refuge to which you can go in the time of trouble, the hounds of life don't worry you much."

Iron Shoes

I think God intended, when he put in the heart of men
the idea of a home, that it should be just this—a place to
which we can go at the end of a trying and haggard day
to renew our strength. I know that in this passage God
realized we would need a refuge when the hour came for
us to wear our iron shoes, and he had the writer of
Deuteronomy to take it down for all the world to read,
"the Lord God is a refuge."

2

The Uncut Pages of Life

These ought ye to have done, and not to leave the other undone.—MATTHEW 23:23.

One day Jesus said to a group of religious leaders, "These ought ye to have done, and not to leave the other undone."

Dr. Louis Banks, an old Methodist preacher, wrote down the best interpretation of the latter part of this sentence that I have ever heard. In substance he said:

One day a boy came to his father and said, "Dad, it's just six weeks before I will be going to college and I was wondering if you were going to give me a going-away present. If you are, I have a suggestion to make."

The father smiling indulgently answered, "What is your suggestion, son?"

The boy's eyes sparkled as he replied, "Dad, could you

find me a secondhand Ford? One that I could take with me and paint the sides crazy-like."

Still smiling, the father replied, "Wouldn't you rather have a brand-new Ford? One that nobody else has ever run?"

The boy's eyes opened wide in astonishment, "Could I have a new one, Dad? Could you afford it?"

Very thoughtfully the father answered, *"Maybe* you *can,* but I'll not promise you definitely today."

The next night when the father came in from the office, he brought the boy a book and asked him as a personal favor to read every page of it. The leaves of the book hadn't been cut. The father called attention to it and said to the boy, "Cut them as you read them." A week went by before the son reticently asked his dad about the car. Immediately the father asked about the book. How far had he read?

"Only about half of it," he answered.

Once more the father said, "Son, please read it all just as soon as you can."

The boy went up to his room and read awhile. As the days went by the boy asked again and again about the car.

Every time his father answered, "I haven't quite decided yet. How about the book?"

And every time the boy would say, "I will go read it right away." Then came the last night before college opened, and the boy sat down on the arm of his father's chair. Seriously he said, "Dad, I don't understand you this time. You and I have always been such pals and we have always been so frank with each other. Tell me why I didn't get the car."

The father responded, "Son, go bring the book that I asked you to read."

The boy stammered a little as he handed it over, "Dad, I read all but the last few pages."

The father took out his penknife and cut the uncut pages, and from between two of them slithered a check made out to an automobile sales company. It was payment in full for a brand-new car. The boy grabbed it and started to dance in glee, and then suddenly stopped and stood very still as it dawned on him that the check had been there for him all along and because he had failed to do what his father told him to do, he had missed the joy of owning the car for a month. His hands trembled as he tore the check into bits and threw it into the fire, and the tears were running down both cheeks as he turned back to his father and said, "Dad, I don't deserve it."

The father pulled him down on the arm of the chair again and spoke these words of wisdom to him, "We miss a lot of things in life, son, when we leave uncut the pages of life that we ought to cut. I believe you have learned your lesson; so we will go get the car. It's been waiting for you for a month, full of gas and oil, ready to run."

How true were the words of that father. When we leave undone the things we ought to do, we miss receiving some of the grandest blessings that our Heavenly Father ever offered. In this passage of Scripture Jesus was entirely in character. He was trying to push back the horizons of people who were religious leaders but who were leaving uncut the pages of the Christian life. Jesus might have spoken these words to Christian leaders today. Indeed, he did speak them and mean them for us. There are some pages of life that we need, in this particular day, to cut.

The first page that so many of us leave uncut is the page of *unreserved consecration.* I am afraid the world wonders just how seriously many of us Christians take Jesus.

Dr. Frank Smith may have been right when he said: "This generation knows little of the consecration that costs anything. We have admired the beauty of Jesus' life; we have acknowledged the wisdom of his teachings; we have used the cross as a symbol in art and worship; but it has not cost us anything in blood, or sweat, or pain."

Could it be possible that we have lifted Jesus up and set him on a pedestal in our churches, worshiped him and left him there? It's a dangerous thing to think of Jesus as an object of worship only. The danger is that we will treat him as the heathen treats his idols, bring him an offering and kneel a little while before him and then go off and live our lives as if Jesus never lived or as if he never died. This is not very far from the picture that Jesus saw when he looked at the crowd to whom he was talking and he said, "These ye ought to have done, and not leave the other undone." True consecration to Christ will mean that we will do our best to walk where Jesus walked and live like Jesus lived. When we bring this down to everyday living, it means that we will accept whatever task, small or great, that will help build the kingdom of God on earth.

Roy Smith has a good illustration of this in his *Sidewalk Sermons*. He tells of two Negroes who were sunning themselves out in front of a country grocery store at the edge of a big woods. One of them was a towering, big fellow of massive frame and bulging muscles. The other was a diminutive chap, very evidently fascinated by the bulk and brawn of his companion. "Man," he exclaimed, "What a man you is! You is about the mos' man I evah seen. Do you know what I would do ef I was as much of a man as you is?"

"What would you do, lil' man?" the big one asked without so much as turning his head.

"Why, I'd go ovah into dem woods an' I would fin' me de biggest b'ar in de woods, an' would tackle him bare-handed an' alone, and tear him jaw from jaw and limb from limb jes' to show what a man I was. Dat's what I'd do," and the little fellow's grinning face bespoke the admiration for the giant that he could not put into words.

Slowly the big fellow turned and looked down on the small one. Then, with a slight jerk of his head he said, "Listen, lil' man. They's plenty of *little* b'ars ovah in dem woods! Why don't you go kill yourself one of dem?"

The second uncut page that surely deserves our careful thought is *the building of spiritual reserves.* Christianity and God are, to too many people, emergency measures. Many of us read that little book by that well-known Hollywood star, Mary Pickford, *Why Not Try God?* This is exactly what multitudes of people do. They try everything else first and then try God as a last resort. God offers to us a continual fellowship. In the warmth of that fellowship, strong spiritual reserves are stored away and a healthy moral and spiritual life is grown. Jesus was talking about reserves when he gave us the story of the ten virgins. He did not call the second five wicked nor did he refer to them even as sinners. He used the word "foolish," and they were foolish because they had no reserves.

One of our great thinkers said: "I get tired of hearing people say, 'I am trying to do right.'" People ought not to have to *try* to do right. They should not have to weigh every appeal that comes to them to do the wrong thing. They should once and for all decide they are going to put Christ in the throne room of their lives and live so that when a temptation comes the decision will be automatic. Temptation should not be entertained nor fondled. This was Balaam's mistake. When King Balak offered him beautiful gifts to come and curse the Israelites, he entertained the messengers overnight; and when he finally sent back the answer, it was neither definite nor dogmatic enough to convince Balak.

Jeremiah also presented this truth on the negative side when he asked, "Can the Ethiopian change his skin, or the leopard his spots?" Then, will a man accustomed to do evil do right?

Surely the converse of this is just as true. A man who is accustomed to living close to God and doing the things that are right, who carries a surplus in his spiritual reserves bank, will not do easily the thing that is wrong. We should stop using God only in an emergency and make him a part of our everyday lives.

A few days after a hurricane, a Miami pastor had a visitor whom he had never seen before. She came to ask him this question, "I prayed as hard as anybody in this town that God would protect my home and my family, but the hurricane literally destroyed my house. Tell me why."

"Are you a Christian?" the pastor asked.

"No, I am not, but I prayed, and God ought to hear the prayer of anyone."

His answer is a classic: "Lady, I don't know why, unless God was busy taking care of his regular customers."

During the depression there was a run on the banks in the city in which I lived. Two of them closed their doors on the same day, but the First National stayed open as usual. That night I went over to see the president of the First National. He was a deacon in the church that I served, and I wanted him to know how deeply concerned I was about the trouble he was facing. I expected to find him upset and nervous, but to my astonishment and delight he met me at the door with a cheerful smile. After we exchanged a few pleasantries, I said to him, "I want you to know that my prayers are with you in this crisis and I'll be pulling for you tomorrow."

He expressed sincere appreciation and then added, "I am not particularly worried about tomorrow; in fact, I think I'm going to enjoy it."

"But," I said, "you surely will have a run on the bank tomorrow, won't you?"

"Yes," he answered, "we'll have a run, but stacked up in the vaults of the First National are more dollars than the depositors can ever check out. We have been expecting

15

this, and our reserves are intact. They will come piling in tomorrow, scared, frantic, and it's going to be fun to stand up there and tell them, 'Take your time. There is enough money here for everybody. You can draw every cent out that you ever put into this bank.' They will draw it out and hold it in their hands a while and then put it back."

I went back home thinking, "What a grand thing it is for a man to have financial reserves and moral reserves and, above all, spiritual reserves sufficient to take care of any emergency that arises."

The third uncut page is well expressed in the words of the three Hebrew children who were thrown into the fiery furnace. Their statement to the king has been set to music and sung wherever the banner of Jesus floats: "Our God is able to deliver us." Paul almost quoted it when he said, "I can do all things through Christ which strengtheneth me." And again we find it in the words, "All things are possible. Only believe." We sing these words and we quote them, but are they deeply embedded in our hearts? Do we really believe that God is able to do everything?

Dr. James Chalmers, missionary to the cannibals in the South Sea Islands, makes our faith look pale as he relates some of his experiences.

"I had set up camp," he said, "in a dangerous tribe of cannibals. Day after day I pled with the old chief to let me preach to his people. I could speak his language and I told him the story of Jesus with all the fervor of my heart. He listened attentively but was not convinced.

16

"I had not paid much attention to his son, who sat just behind him, until one day the son came to my tent with questions that were so penetrating they startled me. The weeks wore on, and I was a virtual prisoner. Then one day toward sunset the tom-toms began to beat and the tribe began to gather and the huge fire was built. Two rough young giants led me into the center of the ring and tied me to a stake. The old chief held his pow-wow and a death sentence was passed on me.

"Wild dancing and carousing followed way into the night. Finally it was stilled by the old chief's standing and holding out both hands. He made a speech to me and added at its end this question, 'Where is your God? If he is able to deliver you, I will believe on him.' My answer was drowned out in the wild yells of delight as the dance was resumed.

"Then suddenly the old chief's son, a tall young giant who carried a long sword that had been taken from a pirate boat, walked into the middle of the circle and stood with his back to me. He whipped his long sword out of its scabbard, and a hush fell over the orgy. In a clear unfaltering voice he said, 'The missionary's God is busy tonight so he sent me to deliver him. There will be no feast tonight. The missionary lives. If any of you objects, I am waiting.'

"A long silence followed, broken only by quiet whispers among the braves. The old chief stepped forward into the circle. The young giant pointed the long sword at the ground in front of his father and his voice was quiet but lethal, 'You may come two more steps. No further.'

"The old chief stopped and stood looking at his son. There was admiration written all over his face. He lifted both hands and turned back to face his tribe and he said: 'Tonight I abdicate as chief in favor of my son. From now on he is your chief. Obey his commands.' He turned and faced his son and said, 'May I have permission to cut the ropes that bind the prisoner?' "

James Chalmers wrote a sentence at the end of that story: "I know whom I have believed, and am persuaded that he is able to keep that which I have committed unto him against that day."

3

Strange Harmonies

Miss Chandler, a great naturalist of 1900, once went
to old Mexico to study the wild life of the mountains.
One morning she noticed a little Mexican wren perched
on a high bough of a near-by bush apparently singing to
the top of his voice. She was astonished at his posture
because she could hear no song at all. Then after a moment the song came to her on a key so high that her
natural ears could hardly catch the vibrations. Deeply
interested, she watched him intently. Then the music
stopped, as far as her hearing was concerned, but from his
position she was sure the little warbler was still singing.

Deeply curious, she went into a Mexican city, borrowed
an amplifier, and set it up close to his nest. A few days

later her efforts were rewarded and she heard the song from beginning to end. She said, "The most beautiful part of the song was the part I couldn't hear with my natural ears." She added that the human ear can hear only about nine and one-half octaves, and that all sound, of course, comes to us by vibrations. A bullfrog croaks below the last key on a piano, and the only time you hear him croak is when he is trying to sing tenor; a cricket chirps above the highest key on the piano, and the only time you hear him chirp is when he is trying to sing bass.

"The human ear," she continued, "has a very narrow range."

Jesus also found that often the human mind has a very small range, and in the Sermon on the Mount he was challenging us all to push back our horizons and let him show us a new world, a new road to happiness—one that had never been tried. Several times he repeated the statement, "Ye have heard that it hath been said. . . but I say unto you. . . ." In this great sermon Jesus was saying to the people around him: "You have missed much of the music of religion. There are many unheard harmonies that you ought to hear. They will add so much of happiness to life."

Very definitely, he told us to *put first things first*. He found a world of men scurrying about concentrating their energy and their thoughts on such secondary things as the raiment they wore and the food they ate and he challenged them to "seek ye first the kingdom of God." The spiritual side of life and the spiritual man, he told them, was far more important than these things. "Seek ye first the kingdom of God . . . and all these things shall be added unto you." Jesus never said "these things" were not important. He never said, "Man shall not live by bread *at all*." Jesus was putting the emphasis on the importance of the proper sequence.

I found a humorous and perfect illustration of this recently. Out in Texas a country preacher had just moved into a new field and was preaching his first sermon in one of his churches at night. During the service some mischievous boys, with the thought of initiating him, changed the wheels on his buggy, putting the low front wheels behind and the high back wheels in front. That night he went to the home of one of his deacons to spend the night.

The next morning the deacon found him looking down the road over which he had traveled the night before, scratching his head in bewilderment. "What's the matter, parson?" the deacon asked.

The parson answered, "I am looking for that hill I came up from the church to your house last night."

"Why, there isn't any hill between my house and the church," the deacon said.

"But," the parson argued, "I know better. It nearly pulled my horse to death and I rode up here on the back of my neck."

When they walked over to the buggy shed a few minutes later, they both broke out laughing. The deacon laid his hand on the preacher's shoulder and said, "There's a great sermon in that, parson. When you get the things in front that belong behind and the things behind that belong in front, you go through life on the back of your neck." How true!

Jesus is saying to us today that we often miss abounding, abundant living because we don't put the spiritual things of life first, where they belong. Jesus added, "He that hath ears to hear, let him hear."

The second thing that Jesus taught which we have had much difficulty in hearing is that little sentence that reads, "Be not anxious about tomorrow." Medical science has emphasized in this generation that being anxious and worrying is one of the most deadly killers of the human race. They tell us that worrying produces an acid that upsets our whole system and burns holes in our lives and subtracts the years from the normal span of life.

A White House physician recently illustrated it this way. He said, "The happiest man I ever knew lived in St. Louis. One day I went over to his home to ask him what was the secret of his happiness.

"A lovable grin came over his face as he asked, 'Have you time to listen to a story?'

"I answered, 'I came over here for it.'

" 'Well,' he continued, 'when I was a young man I was heels over head in love with the sweetest girl that ever lived. I still am and she still is. I have been married to her for thirty years, but she had one fault then and she has it yet—she was always late. One evening just before we were married we were walking down a shady street when we came to a big signboard advertising that a famous singer was going to give a recital in our neighborhood. My sweetheart pulled me up in front of the billboard and exclaimed, 'I certainly would like to hear that man sing.'

" 'I looked at the admission price and said, "But look at the price of the seats, $3.50, and we are trying to save money to furnish our home."

" 'She sighed and we turned away. At the next corner there was another sign and I saw that she was aiming straight for it, so I did a little quick thinking. When we stopped in front of it, she said, "I still would like to hear that man sing."

" 'I pointed out that the price for tickets on this poster was the same as on the other, but I told her that I would take her on one condition, and the condition was that she would *be ready a half-hour ahead of time.* She gleefully promised.

" 'The penalty will be that if you are not ready I am going to tear the tickets up and throw them in the fire."

" 'She answered, "You'll never tear those tickets up, for I'll be ready an hour ahead of time."

" 'When I got to her home about twenty minutes before time, her mother met me at the door and sadly shook her head, "Nellie will never get ready. She just this minute came in."

" 'I walked the floor and I watched the clock as the minutes dragged by and I got more and more furious. Finally, when the half hour was up, I flung myself in a chair by the table and picked up a book. On the flyleaf of it were four little lines that changed my whole life. They read:

> For every evil under the sun
> There is a remedy or there is none.
> If there is one, seek till you find it:
> If there be none, never mind it.

" 'I read it over again with a question in my mind, "Is there any remedy for this?" I came to the conclusion there was none, and that I would never change her. So I decided to make the best of it, just never mind it.

" 'A few minutes later she came hurrying down the stairs. I met her at the foot and with a smile I told her that she was the prettiest, sweetest, loveliest girl in the world.

" 'She froze. "What in the world has happened to you?" she asked, and I quoted the lines to her:

> For every evil under the sun
> There is a remedy or there is none.
> If there is one, seek till you find it;
> If there be none, never mind it.

" 'Smiling, she asked, "So you are going to try that?"

" 'I told her that was my philosophy of life from then on. She held out her hand and said, "Let's shake. I will try it with you."

" 'Still laughing, we ran up the steps to the theater, and the doorman greeted us in a slow drawl, "Don't hurry. The curtain's stuck and it will be a half-hour before the recital begins."

" 'Dr. Barker,' he continued, 'Nothing ever took more misery out of my life than the determination that I wouldn't worry over the things that I couldn't help.' "

It is of prime significance that Jesus devoted a large part of the Sermon on the Mount to this thought. He approached it from two directions. He said, "What man can add a cubit to his height by worrying." Jesus knew that all men wanted to be taller—not necessarily physically taller, but taller in prestige, taller in influence, taller in power, and taller in the minds of other men. He saw around him people scrambling for the high places in life. Invited to a banquet, they strained their necks to see if there was a vacant chair at the head table and with a restrained slowness they hurried for the choice seats. They spent much thought in maneuvering for position. I am sure the Master knew that men of all ages had been and would be spending their mental efforts worrying, striving for "these things."

There was a bit of sad humor in the statement of a young lady the other day when she said, "I am such a good worrier that I have been thinking of making it a profession and charging people for doing their worrying." So many of us form the habit of worrying that we get lonesome without something to worry about, so as fast as we get one worry taken care of we cast about to find a new one.

The other approach that Jesus used was about the fowls of the air and the lilies of the field. He reminded us of a great and vitally necessary truth. He at least impressed it deeply on the mind of one of those who listened to him; for by-and-by, out of the heart of John, the beloved disciple, came these two statements, "Let not your heart be troubled: *ye believe in God*"—and in the midst of Revelation—"the Lord God omnipotent reigneth." The omniscience and omnipotence of God are not just doctrines of our faith. They are everlasting necessities to happiness, to serenity, and to tranquillity. They are great truths in whose presence we can find quietness and peace.

Again Jesus said, "If you ask anything in my name, you shall have it. Enter into your closet and pray." We often sing the song, "Prayer Changes Things," but down in our hearts do we believe it? Is prayer an integral part of our lives, our daily lives, or is it for use just as an emergency measure? Jesus saw the Pharisees out on the street and, recognizing their hollow sham, he tried to make us see that prayer, real prayer, is a necessity of life.

In the *Reader's Digest* recently, a newspaper reporter who was seeking a story about a famous operation that was to be performed was invited by a great surgeon to go into the operating room and watch the operation. When the surgeon had finished scrubbing up and a nurse had slipped the rubber gloves over his hands, he turned to the reporter and said, "Excuse me just a minute." Walking over to the other side of the room, he bowed his head in prayer; for a long minute he stood silent.

When he came back, the astonished reporter asked, "Do you always pray before an operation?"

With a smile the surgeon made this significant reply: "Always. Because I never know what trouble I am going to run into and when I will have to turn the scalpel over to the Great Physician and bid him carry on. Many times in my surgery, when I was at the end of my human ability, God has taken over where I have left off."

Jesus said that we should always pray and remember that if our fellowship with God is kept intact, "As thy days, so shall thy strength be . . . and underneath are the everlasting arms."

4

The Lighter of Candles

Ye are the light of the world.—MATTHEW 5:14.

I had walked around to the back of the auditorium to see if everything was in readiness for the wedding. When I glanced into the auditorium, it seemed that too few lights had been turned on; so I found the bride and told her that I thought the auditorium was too dark.

For a moment she was startled. Then she asked, "Doctor, have they lighted the candles yet?" And I said, "No, they haven't." "Won't you please wait until they light the candles," she said, "and then tell me what your opinion is?"

I replied, "All right," and came back to the auditorium as two ushers went down the center aisle with lighted tapers. There must have been a hundred candles up there, and one by one they lighted them. When they had finished, I stood there amazed, for before me was the most beautiful wedding scene I had ever beheld.

Someone behind me said, breathlessly, "Isn't it lovely?"

And I answered, "It is *now,* but it wasn't a moment ago before they lighted the candles."

That quiet voice behind me said, "So it is the candles that make the difference?"

And I answered, "There's a mighty sermon in what you are saying. It is the *lighted* candles that make the difference." I turned around and said to my unknown friend, "You know, Jesus was a candle-lighter. He was the world's greatest candle-lighter. In him was light. The light was the light of men."

For a minute I forgot the wedding and in thought I followed Jesus along the shores of Galilee and across the hills of Judea. I saw him as he talked to a group of rough fishermen; some of them were mending their nets. Just what he said to them, we will never know. We do know that somehow the unlighted luster of their lives blazed up and each in his own way became a shining beacon. No group of men has ever walked across the world and become such important light bearers.

One day Jesus passed along by the side of a collector of customs and said to him, "Matthew, I need you. Pack up your business and come and follow me. There's a task that your Heavenly Father wants you to do."

I wish we had the details of what followed. I do not know what followed, but I know he closed up his books and folded his tables. I know he made a great supper and invited all of his friends and said to them, "I want you to meet somebody, somebody special." I know that one day he took his pen and wrote the grandest story ever told. Christ, the Lighter of Candles, had touched the little blaze of his taper to the soul of Matthew Levi and it had burst into a glorious light.

They brought a woman who had done something she shouldn't have done and pushed her down in front of Jesus with a question: "Moses said, stone her to death. What do you say?"

Christ looked at her and said something to them that so startled them that they fled in disorder. He turned to her again, "Neither do I condemn thee, Go, and sin no more." Suddenly a new light was in her face and a new and wonderful joy in her heart. She became a messenger of truth.

One day there walked up that road toward Damascus a man that breathed out thunder and lightning, threatening death and imprisonment to the followers of Christ. God touched him with a light and lighted the candle in his life. Then across all of southern Europe and western Asia he went, this giant intellect, ablaze with one great message: "Jesus Christ was God, and he could make a life all over again and put a song in the place of sadness; give beauty for ashes, and laughter for tears."

Nicodemus came and said to Jesus, "You have something I want. Talk to me."

Jesus answered, "Nicodemus, all of your lifetime you have gone through your religious ceremonies as you were taught to do, and you have prayed, read the scripture, attended worship. But, Nicodemus, you need something else. You need to be born again."

Nicodemus asked, "How in the world can I be born again?"

Christ did not go into detail then, but I am pretty sure the hour came when Nicodemus understood what Christ had done. The Lighter of Candles had touched his heart and he wanted above everything else that which he saw in Jesus. He wanted the power to turn the other cheek. He wanted the strength of soul and character to pray for those people that despitefully used him. He wanted the gentleness of Jesus.

This is the message of the New Testament. Probably no other word describes Christ so accurately as the word Light, but we do not need to confine ourselves to the New Testament to see this Lighter of Candles change darkness and gloom into light and loveliness. Look at these three incidents from life.

Some lines written by Paul Laurence Dunbar illustrate it perfectly. There was a day when the gifted Negro poet was cynical and bitter. He was out of touch and tune with everything that was good. To him the world was dark and ugly and the things that happened to him were interpreted in terms of satanic power. Right was on the scaffold and wrong was on the throne when he wrote these lines:

> A crust of bread and a corner to sleep in,
> A minute to smile and an hour to weep in,
> A pint of joy and a peck of trouble,
> And never a laugh but the moans come double:
> And that is life!

And then the Lighter of Candles came by and touched Dunbar's heart. He could not get his poem back, so he did the best he could; he paraphrased his own poem:

The Lighter of Candles

A crust and a corner that love makes precious
With a smile to warm and the tears to refresh us;
And joys seem sweeter when cares come after,
And a moan is the finest of foils for laughter:
And that is life![1]

These words of Abraham Lincoln speak the same message.

On the front porch of his little country store in Illinois, Abraham Lincoln and his partner, Berry, stood. Business was just all gone, and when Berry asked, "How much longer do you think we can keep going?"

Lincoln answered, "It looks like our business has about winked out." And then he continued, "You know I wouldn't mind so much if I could just do what I *want* to do. I want to study law. I wouldn't mind so much if we could sell everything we've got and pay all our bills and have just enough left over to buy one book, Blackstone's commentary on English law, but I guess I can't."

A strange looking wagon was coming up the road. The driver drove it up close to the store porch, and the man looked up at Abraham Lincoln and said, "I am trying to move my family West and I'm out of money. I've got a good barrel on here that I could sell for fifty cents."

Abraham Lincoln's eyes went along over the wagon and came to the wife looking up at him pleadingly, face thin and emaciated, and Abraham Lincoln ran his hand into his pocket and took out, according to him, "the last fifty cents I had" and said, "I reckon I could use a good barrel." All day long the barrel sat on the porch of that

---

[1]Reprinted by permission of Dodd, Mead & Company from *Complete Poems of Paul Lawrence Dunbar.*

31

store. Berry kept chiding him about it. Late in the evening, Abraham Lincoln walked out and looked down into the barrel, and saw some things in the bottom of it, papers that he hadn't noticed. His long arm went down into it and he rumbled them around, and hit something solid. He pulled out a book and stood petrified; it was the commentary on English law by Blackstone.

Now these are his words: "I stood there holding the book, looking up toward the heavens. There came a deep impression on me that God had something for me to do and he was showing me *now* that I had to get ready for it. Why this miracle otherwise?" That day the Lighter of Candles touched the heart of Abraham Lincoln and his life blazed out in glory to do the thing that God needed to be done in the United States of America.

The famous Dr. Edward C. Rosenow, formerly of the Mayo Clinic, is one of the great living bacteriologists. His contribution to the treatment and cure of infantile paralysis alone would entitle him to the undying gratitude of mankind. Why did he decide to devote his life to the patient, laborious study of the cause and cure of disease? Because of a "lighted face."

One night out on an isolated farm in Wisconsin where he grew up, his brother became dangerously ill. When the nearest doctor was sent for, he drove over as fast as he could. Young Edward hid behind a chair where he could observe without being seen. Presently he saw something that determined his career. After careful examination the doctor turned to the parents and smiled, "Have no fear; he is going to get well." Whereupon the pallid, drawn faces of his parents lighted up in a wonderful way to behold, so wonderful that little Edward determined then and there that what he wanted to do more than anything else in this world was something that would cause such light to appear in peoples' faces. What a business! Causing light to appear in peoples' faces.

The message of Christianity does not stop here. It is indeed a glorious truth that Jesus came to drive away the darkness and give us the light of understanding. It is a truth, a glorious truth that he came in order that we might have life, and have it more abundantly. It is likewise a glorious truth that he came to be the Redeemer of the world and make atonement for our sins. But it is a fearful truth that so many of us think of Christianity as stopping right there. So many of our prayers are prayers of petition only. We ask God to give, give, give. To be sure, Jesus told us to ask and we could receive, but he never expected us to stay on the receiving end of life. There was a day when Jesus said, "*I* am the light of the world," but on another day he said, just as emphatically, "*Ye* are the light of the world."

Just as emphatically he told us to "render to Caesar the things that are Caesar's, and to God the things that are God's." He upbraided the Pharisees and the scribes for stopping too soon in the matters of religion. Praying and fasting were not enough. They should have seen the needs of the poor and the widows and met those needs. "With what measure ye mete, it shall be measured to you again." In other words, Jesus was saying, "You must be a blessing in proportion to the blessings that you receive." You must forgive in the same ratio that you expect forgiveness. In the model prayer we read, "Forgive us our debts, as we forgive our debtors." The gospel of Jesus tells us that through his coming we receive another chance, and his whole teachings demand that we likewise give to others another chance.

Dr. A. J. Cronin relates this incident. "My first assignment, after I had finished medical school was in a Welch town and my first operation was a tracheotomy. There was a little girl whose throat was filled with membrane. It was a severe case of diphtheria; so I took my sharp scalpel, and made an incision into the windpipe and put in a tube. I watched life come back and the face lose its blackness, and I thanked God for my training and for his guiding of my hand in that minute.

"Along about midnight I decided to sleep an hour; so I asked the nurse, who was a nineteen-year-old raw, country girl who had just graduated from her training course, 'Do you think you can watch over her and let me get some sleep?'

"She said, 'Yes, doctor.'

"I said, 'Now, you know the tube might get stopped up and you might have to take it out and clean it, then put it back right quickly. You'll have plenty of time to do it and then come and call me.'

"The tube did get stopped up, and she lost her nerve and came running after me instead of taking it out as I had directed. When I got there the child was dead.

"I was so furiously angry that I talked to her for twenty minutes, and the next morning I wrote a long report about why she should have her nurse's license taken away and never be allowed, *never* be allowed to nurse again. I called her in and read it to her. I was fixing to send it to the Board."

He said, "I looked at her as she sat there with her face down, chin against her chest, and a little pity stirred in my heart as she raised her face and looked at me pathetically and pleaded, 'Doctor, give me one more chance.' The tears were awfully close to running down her cheeks, her eyes were full. I turned away and laid the letter down. 'I'll think about it,' I told her. All night long in my dreams there came that same quiet, pleading little voice, 'Give me one more chance,' and I waked up and prayed, 'O Jesus, that's what I had to ask you to do one day, Give me one more chance. O God forgive me for what I nearly did.'

A. J. Cronin writing recently said, "She is today the superintendent of the biggest children's hospital in the British Empire."

Beloved, that's the message of Christianity, "Forgive us our trespasses, as we forgive those that trespass against us." Mercy, forgiveness, another chance, lighting the lights and lives of other people—that's Christianity. Isn't that what you want? Isn't that what *you* want?

5

Life Is an Echo

~~~~~~

With what measure ye mete, it shall be measured
to you again.—MATTHEW 7:12.

Sometime ago I read an article in the *Reader's Digest* entitled, "The Bats Have Used It for a Thousand Years." The article was presenting in everyday language the principles of radar, and in a most interesting way the scientists described a secret that until recently had not been discovered.

It was the secret of how bats were able to fly for miles underground, through dark caverns and never strike the walls. These scientists captured some bats and confined them in a long room, across which wires were stretched.

But the bats in their flight in the darkness of midnight never struck a wire. Then they blindfolded the bats thinking that maybe they were able to see at night. Adhesive tape was put across their eyes; and still they flew with perfect precision, never touching the sides of the room nor the wires. But when they removed the blindfold and taped the bats' ears and their bills, there followed swift disaster. With their eyes wide open they flew into everything.

An amplifier was set up and it was discovered that when a bat began its flight it sang a song; it uttered a shrill, high note, too high for the human ear to detect. The vibrations from this weird song located and positionized any object in its way. The *echo* was the bat's guide. When the vibrations hit anything solid and bounded back, the bat swerved. This, said the scientists, is the principle of radar.

I laid down the article and picked up my Bible. The bats, I thought, might have known it a thousand years, but Jesus recorded it in the Bible two thousand years ago when he said, "With what measure ye mete, it shall be measured to you again." It is a terrifying truth, for there is not one of us who wants to receive measure for measure. This truth tells us that chance is not king in this world, but that we live in a law-abiding universe.

If chance were king, then we might measure out what we pleased to the rest of the world and there would be no reason for it to come back to us. But this is an ordered world, and God at the very beginning laid down the principles of radar in human lives. The Bible expresses it in so many ways that even he who runs may read. We are all familiar with such quotations as: "Be sure your sin will find you out"; "Whatsoever a man soweth, that shall he also reap"; "Cast thy bread upon the waters for thou shalt find it after many days." All of us who have lived a while in this world are familiar with the experience of having an angry word bounce.

Maybe someday we will discover that the word doesn't even have to be spoken but that our minds set up a vibration which reaches the minds of those around us. The very expressions on our faces do set up vibrations and in turn change the facial expressions of others. Some of our fliers recently told of a crash landing in Asia among the savages on the Hump. They couldn't speak a word of the language of the fierce-looking warriors that soon surrounded them.

One of the five fliers, a Major, said to the other, "Smile, smile, smile, and hold out your hands with whatever little personal belongings you can offer as gifts." And the smile bounced and the painted warriors came forward slowly. After examining all the proffered gifts, they returned them and graciously took care of the five injured airmen until some six weeks later they were rescued. One of the fliers said afterward, "There is one universal language—the *smile*."

Dickens tried to express this truth in one of his splendid stories. An old miser was sitting in the counting room of his home, checking his profits for the year. The thought came to him that if his partner were dead, the profits would be doubled. The thought lingered and began to take shape. "Maybe I could murder him and never be discovered," he thought.

As he turned over the plans in his mind, his little

daughter scampered in with a question she wanted to ask, but when she saw her father's face she froze and turned white. She backed slowly away and then fled from the room.

The greedy old merchant sat in amazement. Aloud he said, "Was it possible that she could see what was in my mind? Was it possible that the atmosphere of this room was so charged with murder that it scared her innocent soul?" In terror he back-tracked on his thinking, and it suddenly brought him face to face with the miserable wretch that he was. Like the prodigal son, he came to himself. Like the prodigal son, he came to his Father.

A long time later, as he arose from his knees, the same little daughter, apparently having forgotten her terror, came running back into the room. With a yell of delight she bounced into her father's arms and hugged his neck. "Daddy, please be like you are now, *always*. A while ago you scared me. You seemed so different. Now the room is so bright and full of sunshine. Please stay like you are now." Dickens was saying that even our thoughts may be felt or heard. Vibrations go out from the souls of men.

Now the Bible presents both sides of the great truth. "With what measure ye mete, it shall be measured to you, " for there are definitely two sides of it in life. We are more familiar with the *tragic* side, and the Bible likewise emphasizes the *danger* of it. When Jesus said, "He that taketh the sword shall die by the sword," he was not speaking of the men who made up the armies of the world but he was proclaiming this same truth in dramatic words. The destroyer shall be destroyed; the man who hurts and kills others shall in turn be hurt and killed.

Jacob deceived his old father, and in turn Jacob's children deceived their father. He was paid in the coin of his own realm. He meted out deception and had measured back to him deception.

Ahad wanted Naboth's vineyard, and Jezebel, Ahab's wife, arranged for Naboth to be stoned to death. The record says that "dogs licked the blood of Naboth." When Ahab went for an evening walk in his new vineyard, God sent the old prophet, Elijah, to meet him. The stern old prophet said to Ahab, "In the place where dogs licked the blood of Naboth shall dogs lick thy blood, even thine."

The next time that Ahab went to war, those words were ringing in his ears. In the battle he disguised himself, but a man drew a bow "at a venture" and smote him in the joint of his armor, fatally wounding him. He told the driver of his chariot to take him home. After his death, they washed the chariot and the dogs licked up the blood of Ahab in the same place where Naboth was stoned. And the Bible saw fit to record that when Jezebel was thrown from the palace windows, the dogs licked up the blood of Jezebel. "Measure for measure," the Master said, "is a never failing law."

But there is a beautiful side to this same truth. The *good* you do comes back to you, full measure, pressed down and running over. Likewise, the Bible tells us that when we cast our bread upon the waters, it comes back to us. When you do something fine for someone else, it sets up beautiful vibrations in his heart and by-and-by the fruit of it returns to you.

Listen to this excerpt from "Life in These United States." In one of our American towns there was an auction of city lots that were being sold for delinquent taxes and bringing an average of $600.00 with a few going over $1,000.00. An elderly gentleman, who had been waiting patiently for one particular lot to be put up, opened the bidding with a ridiculously low offer of $25.00. Down in front a soldier, leaning heavily on a pair of crutches, and still wearing his "battle scars," hopefully raised the bid to $30.00.

The old gentleman raised his voice so that all could hear, "If that soldier wants this lot, I will not raise his bid."

There was a hush while the auctioneer waited silently for another bid, then he almost reverently announced, "Sold to the soldier for $30.00."

It didn't take a prophet to see what happened to the grand old man who said, "I'll not raise the bid if the soldier wants it." He realized, as all of us do, that the men who followed our flag in battle really lived a while in hell for us—some even making the supreme sacrifice. Those who came back, whether they were wounded physically or not, carry scars in their minds and in their hearts which represent the suffering they endured that we and our loved ones might yet live and enjoy living. That boy's crutches and his needs started vibrations in the heart of the old man.

Full many a time God lets us wait a while for the measure that's pressed down and running over, but in some way and in God's own sweet time the good comes back to us.

I heard Dr. A. J. Fristoe, one-time state evangelist of Virginia, once say with deep conviction that for every good thing he had ever done in his life he had received from God payment in full, and then he related this experience:

"I went to England on a preaching tour once, and the committee who met me told me that I was to be the guest in one of the finest mansions of the old country and that they had not arranged it but that the owner and his wife had come and begged for the privilege of being my host and hostess for the entire time I was to be in England.

"When I walked into the palace, I was dumfounded and deeply curious. I knew that back of it all must be some reason. I was not kept in suspense long, for as soon as we were comfortably seated my host told me that they didn't feel I was a stranger; for their son had spoken so often of me and had told them so much about me that they had known me for a long time.

"This son was an officer on a British cruiser which had docked for repairs at Norfolk, Virginia, years ago. He had drifted into my church, and because he was concerned about his spiritual life I invited him to come home with me to dinner. He came often after that, and we became fast friends. One day he accepted Christ as his Saviour and I had the pleasure of baptizing him, but I had long since forgotten him, even his name.

"The British newspapers had reached his cruiser on the other side of the world, announcing my coming to England, and he had cabled his father. It was the first time I had ever been entertained by royalty. For nearly two months I lived amidst the loveliest expressions of gratitude"

Dr. Fristoe ended the story with the statement, "Cast your bread upon the waters, and you shall find it after many days."

Let me add the words of Jesus, "With what measure ye mete, it shall be measured to you again."

But maybe the finest reward that comes back to us is the something it does to us inside. Let Edgar Guest say it:

MYSELF

I have to live with myself, and so
I want to be fit for myself to know;
I want to be able as days go by
Always to look myself straight in the eye;
I don't want to stand with the setting sun
And hate myself for things I've done.

I don't want to keep on a closet shelf
A lot of secrets about myself,
And fool myself as I come and go
Into thinking that nobody else will know
The kind of man I really am;
I don't want to dress myself up in sham.

I want to go out with my head erect,
I want to deserve all men's respect;
But here in the struggle for fame and pelf,
I want to be able to like myself.
I don't want to think as I come and go
That I'm bluster and bluff and empty show.

I never can hide myself from me,
I see what others may never see,
I know what others may never know,
I never can fool myself—and so,
Whatever happens, I want to be
Self-respecting and conscience free.[1]

---

1. From *Collected Poems* (1947). Used by permission.

6

Diamond Dust

The Spirit itself beareth witness with our spirit, that we are the children of God: and if children, then heirs; heirs of God, and joint-heirs with Christ; if so be that we suffer with him, that we may be also glorified together. For I reckon that the sufferings of this present time are not worthy to be compared with the glory which shall be revealed in us.—ROMANS 8:16-18.

"I was passing a jewelry store in one of the big cities the other day," said George Strombeck in a *Christian Digest* article several years ago, "and saw in the window a diamond cutter. He had a pile of ugly, shapeless stones on the table by his machine. There were no sparkling blue lights, no scintillating gleams. They looked to be just ordinary stones that you would not have picked up from the pavement. In front of him was a small machine made of two disks about the size of a dinner plate. As I watched, he removed the top one and I saw six beautiful diamonds held by small, sunken clamps. The diamond cutter took out each stone and examined it carefully with his magnifying glass, then clamped it back in place. Then he picked up the box of diamond dust, the hardest cutter in the world, and sprinkled the stones liberally with it. When he had replaced the top disk, he turned on the power and it began to rotate. As I watched, I realized that he was using this diamond dust to shape and polish those dirty, ugly stones and make them scintillate and glow so they would be fit for a girl's engagement ring. As I stood there looking, suddenly my eyes ceased to focus and a great truth took over my conscious mind. It rang like a bell. God, too, uses diamond dust to polish and shape human lives. Some of the hardships, disappointments and frustrations that have come to us are God's diamond dust."

I laid the article down and opened my Bible to the eighth chapter of Romans and read, "The Spirit itself beareth witness with our spirit, that we are the children of God: and if children, then heirs; heirs of God, and joint-heirs with Christ; if so be that we suffer with him, that we may be also glorified together. For I reckon that the sufferings of this present time are not worthy to be compared with the glory which shall be revealed in us."

To be sure, Paul was talking about the hereafter, but I don't think he was talking about the hereafter *only*. He was telling us that the sufferings and the hardships of to-day will "release the imprisoned splendor of our souls." He was saying that God's diamond dust will polish and shape us to be better reflectors of the goodness of God. How true this is of Paul. The writings of Paul are seasoned by his sufferings and the terrible experiences that he endured; he was beaten many times, imprisoned, stoned, and starved. That he endured and still kept the faith, finished his course, fought a good fight makes us be very quiet and still and hug to our hearts the truths that he emphasized. Without God's diamond dust, Paul would not have been Paul. The pages of his life scintillate and glow because of the hardships and sufferings which were his. Because of these things we have been able to see the face of God more clearly through the life of the great apostle.

Now, what does God use for diamond dust on you and me? I can readily think of three things.

Full many a time God uses *the compulsion of circumstances* to polish us and make us finer witnesses and better mirrors for his attributes. Life often surrounds us with a group of circumstances from which there is no escape. They make us prisoners just as Paul was seized, and with them we have to deal. We would like to run away, but, like the little diamonds, we are clamped in and the diamond dust is sprinkled on us.

The day Paul was shipwrecked and went out to pick up sticks to build a fire and a viper fastened itself on the palm of his hand, the people around the fire nudged one another and whispered, "He's a criminal and the gods are not going to let him escape. This is justice."

Paul heard them, and I think he would have liked to have quit. But Paul didn't quit. He kept on picking up sticks and by-and-by the crowd turned from condemnation to adoration. Diamond dust of trying circumstances is one of God's best polishers.

A young ministerial student, from one of the seminaries, found a little church out in the country up New England way that had been closed a long time. There had been no preacher and no services for months. So he went around the neighborhood, found some of the deacons and asked them to let him open the church for services between college sessions. Everybody seemed to be delighted, and there was even enthusiasm when he told them, "There will be no financial responsibility at all. I don't have any place to preach and you don't have any preacher. Just let me come and preach for you this summer."

A group of them met at the church on Saturday and cleaned it up and aired it out. So Sunday morning, a bit nervous and anxious that all would go well, he went over early and was dusting the pews when a broad-shouldered, thick-necked man came in the door and silently looked the church over very carefully. Then he walked on down the aisle to the preacher and asked, "What kind of a church is this?"

The preacher said, "This is just a church that everybody is welcome to worship in. I'm preaching here for the summer."

"Are you the preacher?" was the next question.

"Yes, sir, I'm the preacher."

"Well, can you preach?"

"No, sir. No, sir, I can't preach. I haven't had any experience. I'm just starting out."

The stranger shifted his weight from one foot to the other and said, "I'm an FBI man and I'm up here with President Coolidge. He's in the neighborhood, and he sent me out to find a church where he could worship this morning, and this is the only church I can find. Son, I'm going to bring him over here. Save us a few seats down front. There'll be about twenty of us, and do the best you can."

So the FBI man went out, and the young preacher stood there trembling, perspiration pouring off him. He had five sermons; so he slipped back to his room in a house close by and spread them all out before him, picked out the choice bits from each one of them, and put them all together in one sermon. Then he hurried back to the church. Sure enough, there was the President of the United States and his group.

At the close of the sermon, the same FBI man came up smiling and wrung his hand and said, "You just did fine. President Coolidge asked me to tell you that's the best sermon he's heard in many a month. He'll be up here for five weeks and he'll be here every Sunday." The young preacher's knees gave way and he sat down on the nearest bench.

And the recorder said, "And the boy grew and grew and grew. Coolidge told him at the end of the fifth Sunday, 'Son, God used you. God used you beautifully.'" Diamond dust, just plain diamond dust.

Then again God uses *hardships* for diamond dust. In the *Reader's Digest* of a few years ago, Mrs. William Wallace told an experience which beautifully illustrates this:

"I came into the doctor's office to get my three robust, hardy boys their regular shots before school started. They were romping up and down the hall and I sat down in the doctor's waiting room. Across the room in the corner was a little girl with two crutches. One leg was in a brace—infantile paralysis—but her face wore a happy smile. Hardly had I taken my seat when she said, 'I'm going to walk without my crutches. The doctor just told me so. He just promised me I could walk without my crutches in a few weeks and I'm so happy I just can't wait.'"

" 'Bless your heart, I'm so glad for you,' I answered. Just then the door to the inner office opened and the doctor and the mother came out followed by a little boy. I looked at the mother, feeling sort of sorry for her, then at the boy, and when I saw that he had a withered hand I thought, 'Oh, no, God, you didn't give one mother two of them. No, you couldn't do that, God.' Meg came over, took Pete's hand and they all left laughing.

"Immediately I said to the doctor, as I walked into his office, 'Doctor, a mother with two like that! Oh, Doctor, what a shame. Poor woman, my heart bleeds for her.'

"He said, 'Wait a minute, wait a minute. Just sit down and listen to me. One day,' he continued, 'a girl was on her way up to the state insane asylum to visit her mother who was mentally ill. A boy was on his way to visit his father who was a patient in the same hospital. They met, fell in love with each other and were married. Then they came to talk to me and to ask me if there was any chance of their children inheriting this mental trouble. I told them what I knew, which was precious little. Not long afterwards they came back to say: " 'We want you to find us a little girl. We want to adopt her.' "

"The doctor's voice grew husky, 'Mrs. Wallace, are you listening?'

" 'That young woman smiled at me, "Doctor, don't find us a beautiful, lovely, healthy little girl. Find us one that has a handicap, one that no one else wants. We know what handicaps are. We would like to have one with a handicap and give her a chance." I found Pete for them and they found Meg themselves. And now they've asked me to find them another.' " Diamond dust.

When God needed somebody to care for and look after these, his beloved little ones, did he shape a couple of lives with hardships? Of course, God did not *send* these hardships, but he *used* them. I am sure God's diamond dust is used to shape us to fit his blueprints. Maybe there is no other way but this. Is this what Paul is talking about when he says, "I reckon that the sufferings of this present time are not worthy to be compared with the glory which shall be revealed in us"? Is he telling us that the only way to "release the imprisoned splendor of our souls" is to submit with a strong, courageous spirit to God's diamond dust, to accept without bitterness of soul the unavoidables?

In Baton Rouge, Louisiana, for many years the most lovable woman that the city ever knew took care of the blind and deaf in the state institutions of Louisiana. Both she and her husband were superintendents of two great schools, she superintendent of one, he the other. After his death, she was superintendent of both of them.

One day she said to me, "You know, I wonder just what bearing it has that I lost both of my children when they were tiny little things and my heart full of love for children has gone out to these little sightless, unhearing, unspeaking children until I love them like they were my own."

And I wonder, too, if God in his infinite wisdom, seeing the heartache and the love in her heart, had something to do with it. I do not think God took her children, but I do think he used her indomitable spirit and great trusting soul—polished by the diamond dust of adversity for a task that needed to be done.

Have you ever thought of *prayer* as diamond dust? When we think of prayer, the picture that comes to our minds is a quiet, peaceful, beautiful communion between friends. Someone has defined prayer as friendship with God. Prayer to most of us is a delightful hour. It is the time of pouring out our troubles and our problems to God. It is a time of asking God for the things we need and the things we want. It is a friendly talk with our Father in heaven. This is as it should be, but this is only a part of total prayer. Jesus told us to pray for them that despitefully use us. This is where prayer gets into the realm of diamond dust. Jesus told us to confess our sins, yes, to confess all of our sins. This is not easy, nor is it easy to ask God to help us do the right thing when we have made up our minds what we intend to do.

In the beautiful model prayer called "The Lord's Prayer," Christ demanded that we pray, "Forgive us our trespasses, as we forgive those who trespass against us." Also he told us our prayer should be, "Thy Kingdom come, thy will be done." Each of us has felt at some time in life that it was very difficult to pray that prayer. We too have a will and too many times we would rather pray, "Thy kingdom come and *our* will be done."

In this vein Dr. Norman Vincent Peale has said: "I had a man that sat right down in front of me in church who was about the most miserable man I ever saw. His mouth turned down at the corners and the expression on his face was most unpleasant. I'd come into church and look to see if he was there and then I'd look the other way. One day he came to my office and asked, 'Dr. Peale, why do all the rest of the people in this church look so happy? Are they happy or are they just putting on?' "

Dr. Peale said, "Well, I think most of them are genuinely happy."

"Well, I'm not. I'm just miserable," he answered.

Dr. Peale continued: "I talked to him a long time and found his trouble. He was a businessman and in that particular city he had five competitors and they didn't get along, and he hated them. He came right out and said, 'I wish every last one of them would die tomorrow. They are just no-good crooks.'

"I listened," Dr. Peale said, while he enumerated their faults and then suggested to him, 'Let's talk about *you* instead of your competitors for a while. You told me you were miserable and I've been sitting here trying to diagnose your case and I believe I have it. I know what would make you happy, but you wouldn't do it.' "

He demanded, "How do you know I wouldn't?"

Dr. Peale said: "I *know* you wouldn't. I could tell you what would make you happy and you could get away from being miserable and you'd be just like these other people around you in church, but you wouldn't do it."

He fumed, "Dr. Peale, I will do it. Now, tell me what it is."

Dr. Peale answered: "Well, it's this. Every night get down on your knees and say your prayers and call all of your competitors by name and ask God to bless them and give them more business next year than he gives you."

He stormed back, "I'm not going to do anything of the kind."

"Well, I told you that you wouldn't do it."

"Yes," he said, "and I told you I would, didn't I? But I think you took advantage of me and played a trick on me." So he went on out.

Dr. Peale said: "I watched him as the weeks went by and I could see the transformation in his face. One day he came back to my office, 'Dr. Peale, your prescription works all right. I had lunch with three of them today and I'm going to have lunch with the other two next week. They are pretty fine fellows. I had no idea they were that fine. But, he said, 'Dr. Peale, I've got a confession to make. For a long time after I went away from your office before, when I got down and said my prayers and asked God to bless each one of them, give them more business than he gave me next year, I stopped right there and opened my eyes and looked up and said, "God, you know I don't mean one single word of *that*. But I got to where I did I'm still praying for them and I'm happy.'"

Prayer can be diamond dust. Yes, the diamond dust that God uses to shape us, build us, full many a time is unpleasant. Full many a time it is the unpleasant things of life that bring us into tune and help us to hear what God wants us to hear. Would it not be better to make God's will our will and not wait for God to use his Diamond Dust on us?

7

The Overflow Ministry

And, behold, there was a woman . . . whom Satan hath bound, lo, these eighteen years.
—LUKE 13:11, 16.

Here is one of the most interesting incidents in the life of Jesus. Jesus was in the synagogue on the sabbath day, as was his custom, teaching. The crowds gathered round him, for he taught as one having authority and his words were so different from those of the Pharisees. There was something about him that acted like a magnet and drew men close to him.

Among the church-goers on this particular day was a woman who had "a spirit of infirmity eighteen years." She was bent over, and could in no way lift herself. When Jesus saw her, he stopped teaching and called her to him, laid his hands on her, and immediately "she was made straight." The ruler of the synagogue was indignant. Jesus had broken the synagogue rule by healing on the sabbath day. But the ruler seemed to be afraid of Jesus and addressed his remarks to the crowd, "There are six days in which men ought to work: in them therefore come and be healed, and not on the sabbath day."

The answer that Jesus gave to him is most interesting, "And ought not this woman, being a daughter of Abraham, whom Satan hath bound, lo, these eighteen years, loosed from his bond on the sabbath day?"

Is it significant that Luke, the *physician,* alone records this incident? Does it mean that God needed four separate and distinct personalities to use as a lens for his divine camera when he would give to the future generations a full life-sized picture of his Son? Was there some human element in Matthew's life that would photograph for human eyes some divine characteristic of Jesus that others might miss? Are there Four Gospels because no single personality could answer God's needs in portraying the life of Jesus?

When I look at the Four Gospels, I remember what an old Southern soldier said about the Confederate monument in Richmond: "I have looked at it in the early morning with the sun rising behind it, and it was beautiful. I have looked at it in the evening with the sun setting behind it, and it was beautiful. I have looked at it with the James River as a background, and it was beautiful. I have laid beside the river and looked up at it silhouetted against the sky, and it was beautiful. From no one position could you possibly see and appreciate all of its glory."

So God needed four men, four *different* men to paint a picture of Jesus. Even then, with all their divine inspiration, their picture is incomplete. The words of the Queen of Sheba come back to us, "The half has never yet been told." The portrait of Jesus is unfinished. It's a glorious thought that each one of us "in this our day" has the privilege of painting for the world a little part of the portrait of Jesus. Since each of us is different and each personality is original, it could be that God will let us "paint in" some color that has never been used before. In this beautiful incident there are three messages that stand out above the others.

First, here is a perfect picture of the *overflow ministry* of Jesus. We all know that God gave Jesus two major assignments. One was to redeem the souls of men. The other was to give us the true revelation of God. The Old Testament picture of God was incomplete, and Jesus portrayed him as a *loving Heavenly Father* interested in each one of us individually.

Aside from the major assignments, the overflow ministry is one of the loveliest lessons in the life of Christ. This day he came into the synagogue to teach, to teach men how to live, to teach men about God, and he saw in his congregation the sufferer. He stopped his teaching and, as Moses, "he turned aside." Suffering humanity made him suffer. One day he stopped a funeral and relieved the mental agony of those who wept. Another day he walked through Jericho, and a blind man called to him. The excited crowd around him tried to silence Bartimeus. But Jesus stopped the crowd, called the blind man, and restored his sight. The overflow ministry.

Mothers drawn to Jesus, hungry for something that he had, wanted it for themselves and their babies, asked for a blessing. The disciples would have driven them away, but Jesus rebuked them and gently said, "Suffer the little children to come unto me, and forbid them not: for of such is the kingdom of God." The overflow ministry.

Another day they interrupted him in his teaching to let down in front of him a man with palsy. I think he welcomed the interruption because it gave him an opportunity to ease suffering humanity and to put again into practice the overflow ministry. The picture of Jesus is incomplete without the gentle, tender, overflow ministry. It made people love him then; it makes us love him now.

Here is a great truth that every Christian needs to know. Through the overflow ministry of our lives we will do our finest witnessing for Christ.

One bitter, cold evening just before dark there came a knock on the door of the little house I lived in while at the seminary. The pastor of a near-by church was standing on the porch, his greatcoat covered with snow. He was wearing galoshes and ear muffs.

"Come in," I said to him. "What in the world are you doing out in this zero weather?"

His face was radiant as he answered: "I have just seen something that I have to share with somebody before I go home. There's a little elderly widow living at the foot of the hill. Our church takes care of her. I was afraid she might need something in this bitter, cold weather, so I went to see her. There was a little mischief in her eyes as she took me into the living room where a basket of groceries sat on the table and a man's greatcoat lay across a chair. When I got over my snow blindness enough to see, I said to her banteringly, 'Where is he, Auntie? You've got a man hidden around here somewhere. Trot him out.'

"Cheerily she answered, 'You'd be surprised—no you wouldn't, because you know him. Come to the kitchen window.' Then I heard the ring of an ax, and after we had scratched the frost off the window, I saw the president of the seminary chopping wood under the woodshed." The overflow ministry. Here was a man with an assignment, a God-given assignment, who had turned aside from his teaching to release some of the spirit of Christ that so filled his life. This was one of the reasons, maybe the *big* reason, that every student loved him.

The second message of this incident is the *power of Christ to straighten that which is crooked.* Of course, the incident refers to a physical body that was twisted, bent, and crooked—and it's a glorious message that Jesus can straighten crooked bodies—but it is even more glorious that he can make straight the crooked lives. Both messages are written all over this incident because Jesus himself said of this woman that she was "bound of Satan, lo, these eighteen years."

Here is one of the greatest messages of Christianity, one that needs to be sounded from every pulpit: not only is there "power in the blood" to cleanse us from sin, but there is power in the Son of God to break the bonds of Satan and set us free. Through the counsel room of every minister limps a continual stream of men and women who are handcuffed by some habit, some appetite, some sin, that has made them prisoners, has hung chains too heavy to carry over their necks. They need to know that Christ, God's Son, can lift them up, make them straight, and break the bonds of Satan.

S. H. Hadley, of the Water Street Mission, New York, said: "The most glorious experience I ever had was with an old drunk known as the major. He came into the mission for the last service one night, looked over the crowd, and started for the altar. He knew it was our custom to give a bowl of soup and a night's lodging to those who came forward at this last service and knelt at the altar for prayer. I am sure he used it as a racket and came as often as he dared, just for the soup and the bed. This particular night I was tired and fretful, and it angered me to see him, so I did something I have never done before or since. I met him half-way down the aisle, turned him around and gave him the bum's rush out of the door.

"That night I could not get to sleep. I knew I had done wrong, and my conscience was hurting me. Finally I got up, put on my clothes, and went to find the major. I knew that he would be near by in a flop house or in the back of a saloon. I didn't have any trouble finding him. He was fast asleep on the cold floor of a room behind a bar.

"Then a strange thing happened. I looked into his bearded face and through the dirt I saw something I had never noticed before. I am sure God opened my eyes that I might see what Jesus saw in such men as Zaccheus and Simon Peter and Matthew Levi. I sat down and took the old major's head in my lap. As I stroked his forehead and pushed back his hair, he opened his eyes. With some affection I said to him, 'Major, I am sorry about tonight.

I love you and Jesus loves you. Come on back and I'll give you a bed and something to eat.'

"The old major sat up and looked intently at me for a long time, and then he stammered, 'What did you say, Hadley?'

"I repeated, 'Come on back and I'll give you something to eat.'

"He held up his head and said, 'But what did you say before that, Hadley?'

"When I told him, he hung his head and tears came in his eyes. 'Hadley,' he said, 'no one has used that word "love" to me since my little daughter died and I turned to drink.'

"That night God changed the old major's life and set him free. He lived only six months, but in those six months God used him to straighten the lives of hundreds of men." The same power that straightened the woman bound by Satan still lives in this world. With God all things are possible.

Third, the woman put herself in the *channel of blessing*. Full many a time God's blessings run in channels, and we can miss them if we stay away from the channels. Oh, to be sure, God is everywhere. "And if I make my bed in hell, thou art there." To be sure, there is no place on earth where the presence of God cannot reach a sinner, but isn't it true that many of the most beautiful blessings of Jesus are missed because "we are numbered and not present." This woman might have stayed away from the synagogue on this particular sabbath. Certainly she had a good excuse; no one would have criticized her or blamed her.

People stay away from church for far less, and they miss a blessing, too, because they do not put themselves in the channel of blessings. If she had stayed away this sabbath, she probably would have gone through life bent with an infirmity. I don't think that Jesus ever taught in this synagogue again. In all probability she never would have crossed his path again. Probably as you read, words of a song come back to you—"Make me a channel of blessing today." One of the messages of this passage of Scripture is that we should earnestly endeavor to help others find the channel of blessings.

An old deacon, Brother Holyland, of Baltimore, once told me the story that beautifully illustrates this. He said: "For a long time there were no conversions in 'Old Round Top Church' in my city. Then one Sunday morning five young men walked down the aisle when the invitation was given. The whole church was stirred, thrilled. Sunday night others followed their footsteps. The following Sunday the same glorious experience was repeated at both services, and the pastor was so moved that after receiving the new members into the church, he walked back into the pulpit and said, 'It seems that God is ready to pour out a revival on our church. I am going to preach every night this week.' Then he exhorted us to pray and to come and to do personal work.

"It was a glorious week. On the last morning he asked that if any of us knew what had started the revival please to tell him when the service was over. He had a feeling there was a secret somewhere that he wanted very much to know, but the people left without giving him an answer.

"Then the old sexton came humbly and said, 'Pastor, if

you will come down here at three o'clock and let me hide you, you will get the answer to your question. I'se bound to secrecy, but I'll put you where you can see for yourself.'"

That afternoon the pastor, from his hiding place, saw five deacons come into a Sunday school room, kneel and pray, then talk together about visits they had made and were going to make. When they were ready to leave, the pastor walked out of his hiding place, and apologized for eavesdropping. The deacons were glad, for they hadn't known how to tell him they were ashamed that they had been leaving it all for him to do—and that they had started a few weeks ago to do some personal soul-winning. Those five young men were the results of their first calls. Brother Holyland admitted that he was one of those five deacons.

Graphically this tells us that a few people, a Master's minority, can put a whole church in the channel of blessings.

8

Rizpah

*The blood of Jesus Christ his Son cleanseth us
from all sin.*—1 JOHN 1:7.

Pressed into the compendium of one little sentence in
the twenty-first chapter of 2 Samuel is the heart of one of
the most dramatic and pathetic stories ever written.
Tennyson was inspired by it when he wrote his poem
"Rizpah."

You know the story. There was a famine in the days of
David that lasted for three years, and David asked God,
"Why?" The Lord told him it was because of Saul's
treatment of the Gibeonites. You remember the Gibeonites were a remnant of the Amorites and that the children of Israel had promised them, in the name of Jehovah,
that they would not be molested nor mistreated. Saul, in
his zeal for Israel and maybe in anger, had walked rough-

shod over the Gibeonites. The Lord told David to make amends and atonement and the famine would cease.

David quickly dispatched a messenger to the Gibeonites requesting them to send emissaries empowered to make peace. Smilingly these cunning diplomats from the Gibeonites came in. David said to them, "I want to make amends for what Saul did to you. Tell me what I can do."

Graciously they answered, "Well, we don't want you to give us any silver or any gold. We don't want you to put anybody to death."

David walked head-on into their well-laid trap. "Then, if you don't want any silver or any gold, if you don't want me to put anyone to death, say what you want and you shall have it." Their smiles disappeared, and the teeth of the wolf came out. Their answer must have stunned David, for they asked for the seven sons of Saul that they might take them up to the hill of Gibeah and torture them. The King James Version uses the word "hang." Our old Hebrew professor said, "It probably meant crucify or hang with nails."

They took the seven sons of Saul up to the hill of Gibeah, and runners went out to summon all the Gibeonites. That was a gala day for this little remnant of Amorites. Draw on your imagination a moment and you can see what happened. All day long they paraded back and forth in front of the seven suffering sons of Saul, snapped their fingers, hissed and ridiculed, jeered and sneered. Then the day ended, and the boys were dead.

As twilight descended, a little old woman, mother of two of the sons, a concubine of Saul named Rizpah, climbed the hill of Gibeah. Sobs shook her frail frame and tears ran down her face and dropped into the heath. When she found the two that belonged to her, I imagine she did what any American mother would have done, she kissed their bloody feet and wept her heart out. It was the law that anyone put to death could not be buried, so they had to hang there until, as Tennyson said, "the wind rattled their bones," and the vultures picked them clean, or until the beasts of the forest tore them down. That was their fate or what it was supposed to be.

Night came and Rizpah spread her sackcloth on a rock to rest. But there was no rest for her, for the wild beasts of the forest smelled the blood and, snarling, they had come for their feast. What did she do? Scream in terror and run away? No, she took the sackcloth and flashed it over her head, screaming in defiance, and drove them back into the forest. Day came. Exhausted, she again spread the sackcloth to rest. A shadow, and another, and then another careened before her. Wearily she lifted her face to see the vultures of the air that had come for their feast. Once more the sackcloth flashed her defiance.

Read what the Bible says: "And Rizpah the daughter of Aiah took sackcloth, and spread it for her upon the rock, from the beginning of the harvest until the water dropped upon them out of heaven, and suffered neither the birds of the air to rest on them by day, nor the beasts of the field by night." The barley harvest was in May, and the first rains came in September. June, July, August, September, she stayed among the decaying bodies of the seven sons and drove the beasts off by night and the birds of the air by day.

Then into the silken seclusion of David's palace seeped the rumor, "Poor Rizpah. She is going mad."

David asked, "What's the matter with Rizpah?"

They answered, "Hadn't you heard? They fixed a little tent for her up there where the seven sons of Saul are and she's kept the beasts off at night and the birds of the air by day. She hasn't left her post, they've carried her things to eat."

David, remorseful, his whole heart bursting, ordered: "Take that law off of the statute books *now*. Go get those seven sons of Saul, bring them down here and bury them in the king's burying ground. That's where they belong, all of them." That's the story.

Ask one question. Ask one question of the three groups of people that went up to the hill of Gibeah on that fateful day and this story comes right down to our time. The question is, "Why are you here on the hill of Gibeah to-day?"

Ask it first of the seven sons of Saul. If their swollen lips, parched and cracked, and their swollen tongues could answer, they would say, "Our father sinned. We didn't know anything about it. We didn't do anything. Why, we were just children. Our father sinned."

Dr. Howard Kelly, one of the most famous physicians Baltimore has ever known, once invited all of the ministers of every denomination to come into the auditorium of the YMCA and see two reels of moving pictures. Some six hundred of us met him on that Monday morning. The great doctor walked up on the platform and in a quiet voice began: "My brethren, the pictures that I am going to show you will break your hearts. They are tiny babies born in my hospital, all deformed and shapeless. Not one of them lived very long." The lights went out, and the pictures that were flashed on the screen were horrible. At the conclusion, Dr. Kelly in a husky voice said, "I can write across those two reels of pictures one sentence, "Their fathers or their mothers sinned."

The words of the Old Testament came back to us, "The iniquities of the father shall be visited upon the children from generation to generation." The Lord in heaven knows the physical sins that wreck the lives of children are bad enough, but there are many sins that do not belong to the physical realm that are far more poisonous and insidious than the ones that Dr. Kelly so dramatically pictured. The sins of disposition are as deadly as the venom of a rattler. The psychiatrists are writing, speaking, teaching continually that "sense of security" is vital to the normal development and growth of a child. There is no way to measure the harm that is done by broken homes. There is no way to measure the damage that is done to a child in the malleable stage by the *wrong atmosphere* in a home.

Carey Barker, one-time captain of the Washington and Lee football team, told me one of the most pathetic things he had ever seen. "Just before dark one afternoon," he said, "I was walking down a street in Richmond and saw a chubby little boy sitting on the edge of the sidewalk with his feet down in the street. His elbows were resting on his knees and his face was in his hands. Under one arm was a partially deflated football. He was so pathetic looking that I just walked over and sat down by him.

'Sonny, what's the matter?' I asked. 'Why are you sitting down here like you had lost your best friend?'

"He twisted around and looked at me for a moment and asked, 'Mister, did you ever play football?'

"'Sure did. I was captain of Washington and Lee and fullback for two years.'

"'Then, Mister, you know what it means when a player is off side. The whole team, not just the player, gets penalized. Everybody in the grandstand that's rootin' for them gets penalized. Everybody that's pullin' for them on the radio gets penalized.'

"I said to him, 'You are so right, son, you are so right.'

"After a moment he went on: 'Well, Mister, my daddy is off side. He came home drunk tonight. Mother had the nicest dinner ready. She was singing and smiling and happy as she put it on the table. I was washing up when Dad came in. Mister, he turned the table over and slapped Mother across the face. I sneaked out the back door and came back over here and thought I'd kick the football around a while, but it ain't any fun to kick a football around by yourself. All the other boys have gone home.' "

Carey Barker said: "I stayed with him a long time. I took him out and bought him some supper and then went on my way thinking how the sins of a father or a mother can wreck the happiness of a home, and the happiness of a boy."

It's just a step to the story of the two prodigal sons, the one of them spending his money in riotous living and breaking his father's heart; the other guilty of the sins of disposition, refusing to come in to the feast and likewise breaking a father's heart. When one person is off side, the whole team gets penalized.

Ask the same question now of the Gibeonites, "Why are you here on the hill of Gibeah?"

Back comes the answer through gritted teeth, "Revenge. We are here to settle a grudge. We are here to get even with a man we hated." Here is another deadly sin that in this generation needs to be brought into the open where the light of reason and the words of Jesus can enable us to see its danger. A little grudge, a little grievance nursed, pondered and brooded over, can become a cancer in our souls. We let our imaginations play around it. We go to sleep at night thinking about it until it grows bigger and bigger and wrecks our health and spoils our peace of mind.

A physician friend, Dr. Akins, has told of one of his patients who was in the hospital awaiting an operation. He said: "When I went in to see her the day before the operation, she didn't seem in the least perturbed or upset. She was apparently defiant and very smug. In fact, her whole demeanor puzzled me. She had the appearance of having won a victory instead of any apprehension about the operation. I said to her, 'You are not uneasy about your operation, are you?' "She almost snapped out the answer, 'I am not.' And then continued with a gleam in her eyes: "I wanted a fur coat for Christmas. I tried my best to get my husband to buy it for me. It would have cost him $600.00. He said he couldn't afford it. This operation is going to cost that old skinflint $1,500.00."

Dr. Akins said: "I sat there dumfounded. For a long

time I was silent. I was thinking, 'Poor, poor soul. You don't realize what that resentment has cost *you* in this last six months.' This great doctor went on to say, "There are literally thousands and thousands of people whose physical health is entirely undermined and wrecked because of grievances and grudges that they carry around in their hearts."

Dr. Charles M. Crowe has a paragraph in his recent book, *On Living with Yourself*, that might well be read over and over.

Emerson stated the idea this way: "A man is what he thinks about all day long." Marcus Aurelius summed it up in eight words: "Our life is what our thoughts make it." Here are eight words that can change our lives. It can't be otherwise. The experience of the race confirms it. If our thoughts live in the gutter, we'll be in the gutter. If our thoughts are directed toward the fine and clean things of life, we will walk the earth as the children of God. Pygmy thoughts make little men; great thoughts make big men. For out of the heart "are the issues of life." As a man "thinketh in his heart, so is he." Jesus, of course, was the great exemplar of this idea. He would say that thoughts of jealousy, hatred, self-interest, make men weaklings. He would say that thoughts of confidence, trust, love, make men victorious.[1]

Ask the same question of Rizpah, "Why are you here on the hill of Gibeah?"

The answer comes back in an old familiar refrain, "Because a mother loves." It's a picture that stirs the human heart. A little mother sitting among the crosses on the hill of Gibeah because two of her boys had been crucified there. Just a few miles away and a few days away, if you

---

[1] Used by permission of the publishers, Abingdon-Cokesbury Press, Nashville, Tennessee.

measure by God's great clocks, another Son was hanged by nails on Golgotha, and on Calvary at sunset three other crosses were silhouetted against an evening sky. Ask the one in the center, "Why are you here?" Back comes the answer, "Because a Father loves." "For God so loved the world, that he gave his only begotton Son, that whosoever believeth in him should not perish, but have everlasting life."

But the answer would not be complete, and I think the Master would continue thus, "The fathers and the children of the world have sinned." Resentments and revenge also drove the nails. The story of Rizpah and the story of Jesus have many things in common, and they bring to mind the most beautiful illustration of the atonement that I ever heard.

Dr. J. C. Massee, popular evangelist, was reared in Georgia. He came to Miami for a revival a few years ago, and closed his last sermon about like this: "My mother was the sweetest woman in the world, but she was very strict about one thing. She wouldn't let us boys play on her snow-white feather beds. She prided herself on having the prettiest, loveliest feather beds in Georgia. I so wanted to get up on top of one of them, dive right straight out into the air and sink out of sight in the middle of it. I knew it would be heavenly, but mother firmly refused.

"One day it had been raining. My big brother had ridden his horse out on the farm to see if the drain ditches were open. Mother and I were in the woodshed. She was washing clothes, and I was making mud pies. I got tired of making mud pies and I went in the house. As I walked down the hall and looked in those bedrooms, those big snow-white feather beds just beckoned to me. In a minute I was on the top of one of them. I jumped just as high as I could jump, flattened out and went out of sight with a shoosh! Ohhhhh! It was glorious. For a few minutes I had the time of my life. Then I heard the rustle of skirts, and I looked toward the door and mother was standing there with her hand ominously behind her. I knew I deserved a whipping.

"Just then the window went up on the other side of the room and that big, six-foot brother of mine came crawling through. 'Wait just a minute, just a minute, Mother,' he said. I could see his horse standing outside. He had ridden by the window and taken in the whole situation. That great, big frame of his came down over the top of me, and he said, 'All right, Mother, go ahead, lay it on. I'll take it for him, this time.'

"I listened, but the switch didn't fall, and when I peeped out from under his shoulder to see what was going on, I saw on mother's face the strangest expression. It was beautiful. There was a trace of a tear, her lips quivered a little, her eyes glistened. She was smiling as she looked at him. She said to him, like she'd forgotten I was there, 'You great big lovable rascal. Pick him up. Take him out of the window. Don't come this way. If you do, I *will* switch you both.'

"He picked me up and took me out the window, put me on the horse in front of him, and we rode away."

Dr. Massee said: "The years rolled on. One day I was where my Heavenly Father told me not to go. I bowed my head for the fall of the rod, which I knew I deserved. Then I felt an arm go around my shoulders. I heard that quiet, gentle voice of Jesus say, 'I'll take it for him, Father. I'll take it for him this time.' I opened my eyes, and it seemed that I could see three crosses against an evening sky, and I could hear from somewhere a voice say, 'The blood of Jesus Christ his Son cleanseth us from all sin.'"

It's just a step from Rizpah to Jesus; it's just a step from Jesus here. We have all sinned and we all need the atoning blood of Jesus Christ.

9

Hinds' Feet

***

*He maketh my feet like hinds' feet, and setteth
me upon my high places.*—PSALM 18:33.

The very fact that God wrote this sentence three times
in his Book should have been enough to make me realize
there was a great truth in it. I confess that each time I
read it, I thought of it as beautiful poetry with some hidden message that I could not quite grasp. I tucked it away
for some future study, and then one day Dr. Glenn Clark
broke it wide open. He had written a book entitled, *I
Will Lift up Mine Eyes,* and in the Introduction he gave a
rich experience. A few months later, Dr. Clark was in our
city, and I invited him to preach for us and tell the experience. It was about like this:

"For years I tried to write an inspirational book, but my
muse would stop and my pen would stick in the parch-

ment. I got discouraged and gave it up. It was while I was a professor in a Midwestern college that I was sent to Chicago on business for the school, and I noticed that Marian Graw, who had just written a best seller, was going to review it and tell us how she wrote it. She was appearing in one of the theaters in the morning, and I was on the front seat before time.

"The velvet curtains parted, and, smiling radiantly, she walked to the front of the platform. 'Thank you for coming. It's so generous and sweet of you to listen to my review.' Then in a lovely, modest spirit she gave us the heart of her book. She concluded with this statement: 'I promised to tell you how I wrote it. I *tried* to write it a long time, but couldn't, and then one day a verse in the Scriptures was fulfilled in my life. The verse reads like this, "He maketh my feet like hinds' feet, and setteth me upon my high places." And God did just that to me. I couldn't write it until I got my "hinds' feet," then it wrote itself faster than I could set it down.' She bowed and went behind the curtains.

"I rushed to the stage entrance, for I wanted to ask her more about the hinds' feet. Marian Graw was gone. I couldn't find her. A few months later I came so close to a nervous breakdown that I was sent out to a ranch, not a dude ranch, but a regular ranch out in the West. There they gave me the most beautiful paint pony on the ranch and the fastest. I enjoyed roughing it with the cowboys. One day the foreman invited me to go with them up on Number Six Mesa, which was the highest. And of course I wanted to go. They were going to take some salt up to the cattle. We climbed up on Number Five and rode

over toward Number Six, but I couldn't see any trail up
the steep incline to Number Six.

" 'Dr. Clark,' the foreman said, 'you can't go up Number
Six. You'll have to wait down here on Number Five.'

"When I asked why, he said a thing that was a key to all
my trouble: 'Our horses are chosen because of their sure-
footedness. They have feet like the feet of a deer. They
can climb anything. They track.'

"I said, 'Wait a minute. What did you say?'

"He repeated it: 'They have feet like the feet of a deer.
Watch the feet of my horse. The hind foot falls exactly
in the track of the front foot. Now, walk yours slowly
and watch his feet. They don't track.' " 'I'll wait down
here,' I said, 'I don't want to go up on the next mesa. I
have something I want to think about.' For back to me
had come Marion Graw's sentence, 'He maketh my feet
like hinds' feet, and setteth me upon my high places.'

"As they went on up Number Six, I got off my horse and
down on my knees: 'Lord, I ought to take my shoes off.
I'm on holy ground. You put it on the lips of a cowboy
to tell me what was the matter with me. My life doesn't
track. It pulls against itself. Instead of its perfect rhythm,
it has a tug of war inside and, God, I've known it all
the time, but somehow I just never would look it in the
face. God help me to track. God help me to get my life to
track.' I was cured. I went home, and my book is written. The tug of war within me was gone. There were
peace and rhythm and coordination."

I am sure Jesus had in mind this great truth when he
said, "And thou shalt love the Lord thy God with all thy

heart, and with all thy soul, and with all thy mind, and with all thy strength: this is the first commandment. And the second is like, namely this, Thou shalt love they neighbour as thyself." He knew that if we carried out this glorious first and second commandment, there would be no inner conflicts. Our lives would track and we would have feet like hinds' feet.

There is no repetition here. "Thou shalt love the Lord thy God with all thy heart." That is, Jesus should be king in the realm of our affections. Love is the central theme of the gospel. Love is the chief attribute of God. Love is the center of salvation. "Thou shalt love the Lord thy God with all thy soul"—the seat of worship. The Old Testament commandment, "Thou shalt have no other gods before me" is not obsolete. It is as much alive this minute as it was when God wrote it down on those tablets of stone.

Again, "Thou shalt love the Lord thy God with all thy mind"—the seat of the intellect. Our thoughts should never be allowed to linger over anything that is out of tune with godliness. Also, "Thou shalt love the Lord thy God with all thy strength." The body is the "temple of God." Cleanliness and attractiveness should adorn the temple of God and thereby adorn the gospel. If we add to this, "Love thy neighbour as thyself," we have a life that's balanced and in perfect step.

I once saw in the railroad station in Cincinnati a large mural which portrayed in a startling way this tug of war inside of man. It was a painting of two men wrestling. At first glance it was a puzzle, for the two men were identical. Their faces, heads, physiques were exactly

78

alike. One had thrown the other and was standing with one foot on his neck, the other on his loin. It was, of course, a man fighting against himself. Below was written this thoughtful title, "The Eternal Tug of War."

The classic illustration of it in English literature is the story that Robert Louis Stevenson told of Dr. Jekyll and Mr. Hyde. Sometimes we call this a split personality. The psalmist and the prophet said that God could make our feet like hinds' feet and give to our lives perfect co-ordination. Paul knew all about this tug of war. One day he poured out his heart like this, "For the good that I would I do not: but the evil which I would not, that I do."

But this is not all. The promise is even bigger, for the Scripture added, "and setteth me upon my high places." Very definitely the Old Testament writers imply that there is a connection between hinds' feet and "high places." They seem to be saying we shall reach our highest potential only when our lives track for Jesus. There are indeed logic and common sense in this reasoning. For instance, I saw a car recently that evidently had been in an accident. The rear wheels did not at all follow the tracks of the front wheels. They had been knocked about six inches out of line. As it rolled along in front of me I thought: "Well, it will still serve for transportation down here on the level roads of Florida, but it would never climb Mount Mitchell or Pike's Peak, for its power is dissipated. It's pulling against itself." Then my thoughts turned to people. They too can dissipate their power, be consigned to the lowlands of life, and never reach the high places. Saul was one of these; Samson was another.

Pharaoh could have been a hero. The name of Judas could have been listed among the heroic immortals and have a million namesakes as Peter, James, John, Luke, and Mark. Yes, high places and hinds' feet are closely connected.

An executive in a big business firm gave a splendid illustration of this:

"We tried to set up our business office so that no one person would be indispensable. It worked fine for a while. And then one young lady upset all our calculations. I noticed the office boy dusted her desk more carefully than any of the others, and placed flowers on it every morning. When she came in every morning, all the clerks who were present looked up and smiled a pleasant 'good morning.' There was something radiant about her. Carefully I kept an eye on the office for a few days, and saw one clerk after another find some reason to go and talk to her.

"One day I called her into my office and asked her what was the secret of the influence that she held and the magnetism that drew smiles and attention from everyone. After a little insistence on my part, she told me that it dated from a day when this was not true. She said: 'I took pride in having no friends and being entirely independent. Then one day I realized how miserable and lonely I was and wandered into a church service. The minister was talking about trusting God implicitly and getting rid of our fears and misery. After I got home I pondered a long time on the thought and decided that for one day I would live as though I had nothing to dread or fear about the future—that I would live one day trusting God to take care of everything and set me free. The experience was so glorious I decided to try it another day. For a long time I added day to day. It seemed to me that the office had changed, the people in it had changed—and then I realized that the change had been in me. All the worrying, all the antagonism, all the pride were gone.'" As I read the story, I thought of the deep and close connection between hinds' feet and high places.

There are two questions which come immediately to our minds. First, what causes this tug of war? What keeps our lives from tracking? What breaks the rhythm of our lives? The answer is a small three-letter word, *sin.* Maybe sins of omission, the things we leave undone, spoil our peace and make our conscience hurt. Or it may be the things we do that are wrong, sins of commission.

In one of my former pastorates was a deacon that I loved very much. One day he came to my office and asked me to go into the auditorium and talk with him. We walked down and sat on the front seat. I asked him what was troubling him. His answer startled me: "I can't pray any more. My prayers won't go any higher than the ceiling. The heavens seem to be made of brass as far as I'm concerned." After a moment of silence he said, "Tell me why it's like that."

I told him that the only thing I could think of that would keep me from praying and keep God from hearing my prayers would be some besetting sin, something that I was doing wrong continuously. I asked him if there was something like this in his life.

His answer was an emphatic no. We knelt, and I prayed

earnestly for him. A week passed, and he came back with the same question, to get the same answer, and again we prayed. Four times this was repeated, and then I left that city for another pastorate. Two years rolled by, and I walked out of my office one day and came face to face with him in the corridor. I was so surprised and delighted to see him that I grabbed him by both shoulders and shook him and embraced him and said, "Man, am I happy to see you!"

He exclaimed, "You ought to be, for I've come all the way from home just to see you." When I tried to lead him into my office, he turned toward the auditorium and said, "Let's go in here and sit on the front seat." After a moment of silence he said: "Brother Roy, I lied to you two years ago on the front seat of the church. I came all the way over here to ask you and God to forgive me. I *was* doing something wrong, plenty wrong, that had built a barrier between God and me. I've told God all about it, but I couldn't be happy until I did this. I wanted to come over here and sit down on the front seat of the church and confess my sins to you."

Today he is filling one of the biggest posts of usefulness in a great church. He has his "hinds' feet" again. God has set him upon his "high places." There is no tug of war within his soul. How perfectly this proves that sins of commission can keep us from tracking with Jesus.

Second, how can we get our hinds' feet? And the answer once more is very simple—complete consecration and surrender to God. The best way for me to say it is with an experience. One Wednesday night while I was at college, I went over to Grove Avenue Baptist Church to prayer meeting. I was late, and the visiting speaker was already bringing his message; so I never knew his name. He was an elderly man with a long white beard, and snow-white hair. His face beamed with radiance. He closed his message with this incident from his life:

"I was pastor in a small church in the valley of Virginia and very happy, because the congregations and the finances were good. Then one Saturday afternoon I answered a knock at the door and found a colporteur, a young ministerial student. Pathetically he told me that he had not sold a book all week and he was without money and very hungry. He asked if I could let him sleep somewhere until Monday, when he would start out again. As I talked with him that night I realized that he was a choice soul, filled with the spirit of Jesus. I invited him to preach for me the next morning, and then I made one of the biggest blunders of my life. I halfway apologized to the congregation for him. I told them we must let these young preachers practice on us, and urged them to give him prayerful and sympathetic attention.

"Then something close to a miracle happened. Hardly had he started preaching when we forgot he was there, for it seemed to all of us that Jesus himself was talking to us. On the way home I asked him, 'How did you learn to preach like that?' "His answer was a question, 'Have you surrendered your life completely to Jesus?'

"Of course, it offended me. How could I be the pastor here without surrendering?

"He immediately apologized, but I knew that God had sent him to put his finger on my life. My surrender was

83

not complete. That night I told my wife I wanted to stay up a while. I had something to talk over with God. My study was a battleground. In my anguish I actually got down on my face and tore the carpet up with my fingernails, but God and I won. I did not go to bed, and the next morning, when I looked into the glass, it seemed that my face had actually changed. I don't know about my face, but the inside of me was changed. You all know I have been the pastor of some of the biggest churches in the world since then and life for me has been glorious."

You might write across his story in big, bold letters, "He maketh my feet like hinds' feet, and setteth me upon my high places."

10

Keeping Life's Windows Clean

In one scene of an old drama called *Windows*, an aged
window cleaner is washing the windows in the library of
a journalist. And as he cleans he talks aloud, apparently
to himself, but in reality to the journalist who is sitting at
his desk lost in thought and holding a pencil idle above a
sheet of paper.

The old window cleaner begins: "People's bedroom winders gets dirty." And as he washes on a little, he peeps
over his shoulder to see if the journalist is annoyed. He
doesn't seem to be, so the old man continues: "People's
hall and dining room and their living room winders gets
dirty. They gets dirty with soot and dust and grease and
smoke. And you can't see out of them very well. It

makes all the world look drab and dull and dim." He continues washing a little while and peeps again over his shoulder. This time to see if the journalist is listening. Satisfied that he is, he says the thing that he set out to say: "People's life winders gets dirty, too. They gets dirty with envies, jealousies, prejudices, and greed, and all of life looks dull and ugly and you don't see things as they are. Sometimes you can't see them at all."

And the author never said a truer thing than this in all of his books. Our life's windows do get dirty and we can't see things as they are. When I read this scene, the story of Balaam and Balak flashed into my mind immediately. Balak was frightened, for the Israelites were flooding across the great plateau and the valley below him. In numbers they were as grasshoppers. Quickly he sent a bribe to Balaam with a request that he come at once and lay a curse upon them. When Balaam came, he told Balak frankly, "I'll have to say exactly what God tells me." So instead of cursing them, he blessed them. This made Balak furiously angry, and he took Balaam to another place where he could see "only a little part" of the moving multitude. The majestic sight of the great throng was hidden from view. He said to Balaam, "If you can see only a little part of them, maybe you can curse them." This was good psychology, for it is when we see only a part or just one side of a thing we often get very perturbed and aggravated. We need to keep our windows clean enough to see the whole and see it as it is. Maybe this is what Jesus had in mind when he said, "Ye shall know the truth, and the truth shall make you free." There are three windows that we should carefully keep clean.

First, the *horizontal* windows. Through these windows we look out on the world around us. Through these we see the sunsets and all the beautiful things that God has created. Ole Bull once played his violin before his king. When he had finished, the king sat very still in meditation for some minutes and then asked Ole Bull a searching question, "Where did you hear the sounds and the music that you have just played?"

With a smile, Ole Bull answered: "You are very discerning, your Majesty. No one else has ever asked me that. I sat in the mountains of our Norway and listened to the mating calls of the birds and caught them in my violin. I listened to the little brook tumble down the mountain singing its murmuring music and caught it in my violin. I listened to the leaves clap their hands in the evening breeze and caught it in my violin. I listened to the storms roll up out of the sea, the crash of thunder, the scream of the wind and caught them in my violin." Do we keep our windows clean enough to see these glorious things that God has made?

Through these windows that look out, we can see the humorous things that happen in this world. God made us so that we could laugh, and he told us in his Word that "a merry heart doeth good like a medicine." We need to keep our sense of humor. Woe unto the man who loses his sense of humor and can't laugh some things off and can't keep laughing even when things go wrong. We are going to *have* to keep our sense of humor. As Will Rogers put it, "God has filled up our world with funny things." And Will was teaching us to see some of them. It is so easy to see the sad things, the terrible things. Why does

87

bad news travel so speedily while funny things lag and good news moves like a funeral march? We should keep our windows clean to see life whole around us.

I am sure some of you remember Dr. Spilman, that little secretary of the Baptist work in North Carolina, who was very, very large around, and very, very short. One day, after we had listened to two or three speeches at a convention, and everybody was tired and hot and worn out, it came time for him to speak. And I thought, "Well, I would certainly hate to have the assignment of speaking now."

Out onto the platform he waddled (that's accurate, he waddled) and lifted up his hands and stood on his tiptoes. Everybody got very still. He began with his voice in a high key, "Ladies and gentlemen, if you can't see me standing up, I'll lie down." And the crowd broke into a roar of laughter. We were rested and ready for the splendid message that he brought. Now, the world is just full of funny things, and that window that looks out on the world needs to be kept clean.

Again, through these windows that look out we can see the open doors of service to a needy world. I was listening to the president of Kiwanis International as he addressed a large group of men in Jackson, Mississippi, not long ago. He closed his talk with a stirring incident out of his experience.

In substance he said: "I came down out of my office one bitter cold afternoon. There was a mixture of snow and rain and sleet, with gusts of wind whipping it everywhere. I turned my big coat collar up and ran for my car. Out of the tail of my eye, I saw a boy backed up into an empty store front. I couldn't go on. I had to turn around and come back. His nose and hands were blue with cold and he was shivering all over.

" 'What's the matter, son?' I asked.

"Quickly he answered, 'Nothin', mister.'

"I tried to smile as I said, 'I've got some boys of my own, son, and I know when there is something the matter with a boy.' His lips trembled a little, 'Mister, my daddy gave me a list of groceries and a dollar bill and sent me to the store. I guess my hand was so cold that the dollar bill blew out without me knowing it and all I have is the list of groceries.' I told him to go on home and tell his daddy what happened and that he would understand.

"The boy shook his head, 'You don't know *my* daddy. He will purt nigh kill me, for he's half drunk. I'm gonna wait till he goes to bed.' 'You can't do that, son,' I said. 'It's getting colder every minute and you will freeze to death. Where is the grocery store and where is your list?' He held up the list and pointed with a trembling finger toward the store. 'Come on,' I told him, 'I'll buy them for you, for I can't go home and leave you out here in the cold.'

"As we walked along, his faltering voice came over the wind, 'I don't know when I'll ever get a dollar to pay you back, mister.'

"I blurted out, 'I don't want you to pay me back. I just want you to go home.'

"The bill was ninety cents; so I gave him the dime and told him not to tell his father anything. He took the bag of groceries and got as far as the door before he stopped and looked back. Then he set the groceries down on the floor, came back and put his arms around my waist, that is, as far as they would go around."

Right here the big president stopped and pulled at his collar, for his emotions were choking him and his voice was getting pretty husky, "You know what that boy said to me? 'Mister, I wisht you was my daddy. I wisht you was my daddy.' You know what I did? I went around three or four blocks in the sleet and the snow to see if I could find another boy that had lost a dollar."

Shouldn't we watch our horizontal windows and make sure they are clean enough to see the pathetic needs of those around us and the golden opportunities of service?

Second, the window that looks *in*. Dr. Cortland Myers, former pastor of Tremont Temple, said: "Let me be fanciful for once. There is a little room in every one of you that might be called the 'holy of holies.' This is where the real *you* lives. No one else is ever allowed into that room. A little weaver sits there in front of a loom and the shuttle moves backward and forward all day. He is weaving the warp and the woof of your character, and he is weaving it out of your thoughts. If the thoughts are pure and beautiful, the shuttle carries white and gold. If the thoughts are ugly and dark, the shuttle is carrying black threads. He uses whatever you put into the bin. Your air castles, your day dreams, your night dreams go into your character."

This is what Jesus meant when he said, "As he [man] thinketh in his heart, so is he." We should keep our windows clean that look into this little room. We should scan carefully the pictures that our imagination hangs on the walls. Our thought habits are so important to our happiness. Dr. Norman Vincent Peale illustrates it with an experience. He said: "I went into the diner for breakfast one morning on one of the fast trains between New York and Chicago. The steward placed me opposite a man and his wife. The husband and I were having a delightful conversation when his wife said, petulantly, 'This grapefruit is bitter. It isn't fit to eat.' A moment later she interrupted the conversation again with some complaint about a cold draft. When she interrupted the third time with another complaint, her husband said, 'Don't mind my wife's complaints, for she is a very fine person. In fact, she is very clever. She is a manufacturer.' A bit astonished, I asked, 'What does she manufacture?' Still smiling, 'Unhappiness,' he answered. 'Her own.'"

The third, of course, is the window that looks *up*. How necessary it is for us to keep the window clean that looks up—the window between us and God. Dr. Charles M. Crowe, in his splendid book,*On Living with Yourself,* has a magnificent page on this subject.

We actually shape events by controlling our thinking. We manage life by controlling it from within. We ourselves become manageable as we discover the poise that comes from mental self-discipline. We must set up an inner kingdom of the mind where the power of our will is sovereign. In such a kingdom we are not pushed about by our feelings, our angers, our unhappy circumstances. In such a kingdom we are strong enough to control our tempers, our hopes, our ideals, because we control our thoughts.

R. L. Williams, president of the Chicago and Northwestern Railroad, tells an interesting story on himself. It was in the early days of his first job with a railroad. He was promoted to the ticket window. He was just a boy, and he felt his importance. He began to think high and mighty thoughts about himself. He developed the habit of being brusque and sarcastic. He liked to be rough and tough with the customers. One day he tried it on a traveling man. The man leaned across the counter and said to him, "You'll have to be courteous, sonny, if you expect to get anywhere. You're going to need friends, and a smart aleck makes nothing but enemies. Get wise to yourself." So young Williams began to experiment with controlling his temper. He pretended to like people. It was a pose at first, but to his surprise it worked. The experiment at controlling his thoughts and attitudes became a habit and then a pleasure. Today he says: "I am convinced that this incident changed the course of my life. Every important advancement I have ever had was implemented by friends."

Have you ever come to the evening when you couldn't say your prayers? Have you ever said to your minister or to yourself, "My prayers don't go up"? Full many a time it has been said to me, and I just didn't have the courage and the heart to answer: "You have gotten your windows dirty between you and God. You have gotten your windows dirty. You know that you have done something that you shouldn't have done. You have let your imagination and thoughts dwell on impure things and the windows between you and God got dirty, and the music went out of your soul." There is only one way to find contentment and happiness, and if you would love life and see happy days, there must be fellowship and sweet communion between your soul and your Saviour.

I once heard Carter Helm Jones in Philadelphia say: "In my home in one of my pastorates I had a prayer room—the Sky Room we called it. It was in the very top of the house, a kind of attic. It was used only for prayer and meditation. One day I came in irritated and fretful. I had been hurrying from one appointment to another. I said to my wife, 'I am going up to the Sky Room and please don't let anybody interrupt me.' It was not necessary to add that last exhortation as my wife was always glad to see me go up to the Sky Room. I was different when I came down. I dragged up the steps, shut the door, and sat down by the little table—the only furniture in the room was a chair, a table, and a Bible. As I idly turned the leaves of the Bible, I heard footsteps tapping on the stairway outside, and then there was a timid knock. A bit irritated that somebody had slipped by my wife's vigil, I opened the door with a frown on my face to find my little six-year-old girl standing there twisting her hands because she knew she had disobeyed. "'Daddy,' she said, 'you've been so busy these last few days that I haven't had time to love you and I want to love you just a minute.'"

He said: "I dropped down on my knees and she put her little arms around my neck and kissed me, and whispered to me, and then slipped out quietly. I just reached over and pushed the door shut without even getting up and said, 'God, I have been so busy going to and fro and up and down on the earth that I haven't had time to love you any. I want to stay here a while just to talk to you.'"

He said beautifully the thing that I am trying to say—that we ought to keep our windows clean between ourselves and God and our fellowship with God warm and glowing.

If there is some sin in our lives, the blood of Jesus Christ cleanses from all sin. If there is something there that needs forgiving, God's mercy is unstrained.

11

The Second Mile

Whosoever shall compel thee to go a mile, go with him twain.—MATTHEW 5:41.

There is an innocent sounding sentence in the Sermon on the Mount spoken by Jesus that contains enough dynamite to change the course of the world. In it Christ has presented one of the foundation principles of abundant living. What a pity that people have gone by on the other side and left this little sentence, with its mighty truth, alone. It reads "Whosoever shall compel thee to go a mile, go with him twain."

Somewhere I read of a Sunday school teacher who had assigned this passage for memory work one Sunday. When the class assembled the next Sunday, being a very understanding and considerate teacher, she repeated the verse to refresh their memories. "Whosoever shall compel

94

thee to go a mile, go with him twain." Then she waited just a moment and asked, "Does anyone know the memory verse?" Up went a hand. "All right, what is it?" The little boy answered, "Whosoever shall compel thee to go with him one mile, go with him *by train*."

The background and setting of the verse are very important. Whenever the Roman Empire had conquered a new province or a new town, a Roman yoke was put in the market place or in the principal gate of the city. Sometimes they made everybody pass under it; sometimes just the leaders of the people, thus signifying and promising that to the Roman Empire they would give obeisance, obedience, tribute, and many other things. One of those "other things" that would be found in the small type was this.

Whenever a Roman soldier or Roman official wanted you to carry his pack for a mile, or run an errand for a mile, or guide him for a mile, it was a must. This was a most humiliating and chafing experience for, as Moses said, "these were a stiff-necked people, a proud people." I have read that the Roman Empire stipulated that except in an emergency no one would be required to go farther than a mile. I've also read that every Jewish boy who lived in the country had marked off a mile each way on the road from his house and had driven a peg down.

Now, with this in mind, look at this group standing around Christ. I imagine that no one thing that Jesus ever said, as he walked the streets of Jerusalem or the roads of Galilee, upset an audience of his like this sentence did. They're listening intently, looking at one another, and marveling at the way this teacher pronounces the great truths. Then suddenly into their midst he drops this bomb, "Whosoever compels thee to go a mile, go with him twain."

I can see them clench their fists until their nails dig into their palms, nudge the man next to them, and shake their heads and look at Jesus in astonishment. Does he mean to say that he approves of the Roman Empire, and that he is teaching that they should obey when they are made to go even one mile? What in the world is the matter with this man? Nothing Christ ever said shocked them so.

I think that Jesus deliberately made that obnoxious Roman rule a carrier for this great principle of life so that they would never overlook it and so we wouldn't miss it. It would be tragic to miss the message of this verse of Scripture. It's tragic for your individual life, your business, or your profession to overlook this truth in the teachings of Christ. What does it mean? Certainly not literally go another mile, carry a pack for another mile. No, it means do just a little more than you are required or reasonably expected to do. In the Sermon on the Mount he was talking about happiness and the abundant life. The whole Sermon was about this, and you cannot have abundant life without practicing the second mile. There are four observations about this second mile that are worthy of our attention.

First: The second mile always leaves a deposit of happiness in the heart of the one who travels it. Let me illustrate it. A famous physician for many years operated in an amphitheater in the city of New York. Many surgeons from all over the country spent their vacations or part of them just watching him from their high seats overlooking the operating table. One day, when he had finished an operation and was taking off his mask, and the other doctors were leaving, one young man dropped down to the operating floor and hesitatingly approached the great surgeon, "Doctor, may I ask you a question?"

"Certainly, son, what is it?"

"Doctor, doesn't medical science say, and do not the books teach that one knot tied in the thread after the operation, if tied correctly, is all that's necessary?"

A genial smile broke over the countenance of the grand old surgeon as he put his arm around the young doctor. "Son, medical books say exactly that. Medical science teaches that. I know what your question is going to be. You're going to ask me why *I* tied *three* knots in that thread after I finished sewing up the wounds, aren't you?"

Smiling, he answered, "Yes, doctor, why three?"

"Son, I'll tell you a secret, since everybody's gone. That third knot is my 'sleeping knot.' I'm going to wake up in the middle of the night tonight and think about this operation, run through it quickly, come down to the end of it, and wonder if I tied the thread tight so the wound couldn't possibly come open, and I'm going to remember I didn't tie *one* knot, I didn't tie *two* knots, I tied *three* knots. It can't come loose, so I'm going to smile and turn over and snuggle down in my pillow and go back to sleep. That's my 'sleeping knot.' And, son, let me tell you a great principle of life. I'm not being original, but

Iron Shoes

if you'll always tie three knots where you're required to
tie one, you'll find a lot of happiness that you can't find
any other way. It's a great principle of life. It applies
to everything."

I don't think this is overdrawn. Here's a Jewish boy
working in his field. A Roman soldier comes along and
calls to him, "Come, carry this pack of mine. I'm tired."
The Jewish boy looks at him. He wishes he could hit him
over the head with the hoe he is using. He slams the hoe
down, slowly drags his feet and creeps over the fence,
chain lightning leaping from his eyes. He picks up the
Roman soldier's pack, half drags it, half carries it, slows
the Roman soldier down, gets to the mile post, slams it
down. "I hope some day I'll meet you when my nation's
on top. I'll make you carry a ton ten miles." He goes
back, picks up the hoe and breaks it against a tree, goes
home and takes it out on his family like a modern man.

Now, here's another one. He's been with Jesus and he's
caught the beauty of this second mile and he's seen the
depth of it. "Come, carry this pack a mile," a Roman
soldier commands. The young man vaults the fence, picks
up the pack and outsteps his Roman soldier, chats with
him, and passes the mile post. By-and-by that Roman
soldier stops and smiles: "Wait a minute. You're too
fine for me to take advantage of you. You've come a long
way past the mile."

And to his amazement the young Jewish boy answers:
"O let's walk on. I'll take you to the edge of the city.
I'm enjoying talking to you. Tell me some more about
Rome. I've some more questions I want to ask you."

The Second Mile

Now, watch that Roman soldier when he gets to the edge of the city. He slips off his grooved glove, thrusts out his hand: "Young man, I'll think a lot more of your nation from now on. If you ever need a friend in the Roman army, I'd like to help you. You've helped me to day."

Now, watch that boy as he goes back, head up, shoulders back, whistling a merry tune. Oh, he's happy inside. What's happened? He's conquered something. An hour of self-approval is worth a week of ordinary living. He picks up the hoe and does two hours' work in one. He goes over the hill, and the children see him coming and they run and tell their mother and she meets him out there. She slips her arms around him and says: "I know what you've done. You've gone the second mile today. It always makes you so much sweeter. It does something wonderful to you."

Second: The second mile calls for the best in others. You can't possibly travel the second mile without influencing others and starting them to traveling it. Let me tell you about the first time I ever saw it. I shall never forget it. I was working as night secretary in a railroad YMCA. A new general secretary had taken over. He redistributed the work and gave me the books to post at night. I never did like to keep books and I resented his giving me this extra work. And every single page of those books showed that I resented it. For the first few months it was just written all over them. I'm afraid they were the ugliest set of books ever kept.

Then one day something happened. I asked the new

secretary, Mr. Goodwin, if I could go hunting, bear hunting with our gang and my dogs. They were going back up into the "bear loop" day after tomorrow. "Would there be any chance for me to get off tomorrow night?"

He thought a moment and answered with a smile: "I think so, Roy. One of us will have to work overtime for you, but I believe we can arrange it all right. I'll just work for you myself. Go ahead and kill a bear."

So I went with the gang and the dogs and hunted for two days. We slept on the mountain that night, and I got back just in time to go to work the next night. He could see how tired I was, and after a while he came over, and, with that same fine smile, he puts his arm around my shoulders and asked, "How many miles did you walk in the last two days? Aren't you pretty tired?"

I answered, "Yes, sir, but I'm all right. I can work through the night."

He said, "Well, I worked for you last night and I'm not a bit sleepy, for I slept all day." And then sort of confidentially, "Slip upstairs and go to bed, and I'll wake you up by-and-by. You sleep till I come and get you."

He told me just once and I was gone. When I opened my eyes next, it was day. I wondered what in the world had happened. Had I gone to sleep on duty? Then I remembered and hurried down to the office. Mr. Goodwin had gone home, but the day secretary handed me a note that he had left for me. I never shall forget that note.

DEAR ROY:

I came up and looked at you, but you were sleep-

100

ing so soundly that I didn't have the heart to wake you. I didn't mind working for you at all. It wasn't a hardship. Don't feel bad about it. Go on home, get your breakfast, and come on back and work for me till noon while I sleep a little. You come back on tonight and we'll all be straightened out. I really enjoyed working for you, Roy. Maybe you haven't found it out yet, but I love you.
It was signed "Manley Goodwin."

I sat down, read the note over. I read it two or three times; then I got down on my knees. I asked God to forgive me for the way I'd treated a good man. I asked him to forgive me for the way I'd kept those books. Now, if you want to see the prettiest set of books that ever were kept, you'll find them in that YMCA. It's written all over them—the second mile that Jesus talked about. That's the first time I ever met it; that's the first time I ever saw it. But I'll be indebted for a lifetime to the man who lived the second mile for me that first time. That's the thing Jesus is talking about, "Whosoever shall compel thee to go one mile, go with him twain." And remember that when you walk that second mile, you start somebody else down the same beautiful road.

Third: The second mile lightens life's burdens. The second mile is one of the grandest principles that Jesus ever gave for felicity in the home. I honestly believe that if one person in a home would practice this second mile that Jesus is talking about, he alone, or she alone, could transform a home. And how many homes would be inviolate today if people practiced the second mile, doing a little more than they were expected to do, a few nicer things than anybody had a right to ask them to do.

If you had a visitor in your home, and were going to give him a glass of milk, you wouldn't skim the cream off first—but that's exactly what we do with one another. Instead of going the "love mile," as Jesus is expressing it here in this passage, we subtract something that is vitally important. Here's a husband hurrying to get ready to go to work in the morning. His wife is washing the breakfast dishes. He finds that he has a button off his coat, and he comes to the kitchen door and says, "Honey, I've got a button off. Can you stop and sew it on?"

Why, of course, she's going to stop and sew it on, but she stops and stands still for a minute. "Your buttons can get off in the most inopportune times. Why didn't you tell me last night it was off?" But she dries her hands, and sews it on. She fusses a little bit as she does, then throws his coat on the table, "There it is. Next time tell me when it gets loose." She goes on back to her dishwashing. Toward the end of the week, the wife says to her husband, "I had a little extra expense this week and my budget's running short. I'm going to need about five dollars more." He turns around with a glare, "What in the world do you do with all of your money anyhow?"

Let's see what this second mile would do for that home. "Honey, I've got a button off. Could you sew it on?"

With a smile she dries her hands and hurries to get a needle and thread: "You know, sweetheart, I just love to sew buttons on for you. I'll have it on in just a minute."

When she has finished, she holds the coat for him, her arms go around his neck and she gives him a little hug. He goes away to work with a song in his heart thinking she's the grandest woman that ever lived. And she is. At the end of the week: "Honey, I've had a little extra expense and my budget's about five dollars short."

Out comes his wallet and he says, "I don't see how in the world you ever make money stretch as far as you do. Here's ten dollars instead of five."

Now, you laugh about it, but oh, the difference it would make in the atmosphere of our homes if the people in them would do a little more than is expected of them, were just a little nicer, just a little kinder, just a little sweeter than anybody had a right to expect them to be. Our children would grow up in an atmosphere of joy and good will. What a difference it would make in their lives and the way they would face the problems of the world. The second mile is just crammed full of blessedness.

Fourth: God went the second mile. Jesus never gave us a commandment that he himself did not live. Of course, the greatest second mile ever presented to the world was Jesus himself. God created a beautiful world, filled it full of lovely conveniences which would add to our happiness. He gave us a Guidebook and a thousand things to remind us of himself and all of his goodness. Despite all this, man turned away from God. Then God went the second mile, and sent us Jesus, and told John to write it down, "For God so loved the world, that he gave his only begotten Son, that whosoever believeth in him should not perish, but have everlasting life."

The day came when Jesus was hung on the cross on Golgotha. They had driven the nails in his hands and feet and left him to die in agony. In the midst of it all, he lifted his face quietly up to his Heavenly Father, "Father, forgive them; for they know not what they do."

I saw the Passion play at Oberammergau the last time it was played. The dramatist added a few scenes to the account given us in the New Testament. One of them beautifully illustrates this truth of the second mile. Jesus was carrying his cross down the streets of Jerusalem. The end of the upright beam dragged on the ground behind him. He staggered and fell. The crowd jeered. A Roman soldier struck him. A centurion who was in charge of the procession carried a long vicious whip. He quickly uncoiled it and swung it out over his head and brought it down with a resounding crack, not across the back of Jesus, but across the back of the soldier who struck him. "Help him up," he commanded, "And don't strike him again." I've loved a Roman centurion ever since.

Just then from the other direction came the mother of Jesus and a group of women. The centurion rode his horse out in front of the crowd and stopped them and told Jesus to go and talk with his mother. For a long time the two wept silently in each other's arms, and when Jesus went back to the cross he couldn't lift it. Just then Simon of Cyrene, who was short and stocky and strong, came up a side road and stopped to look at the scene. The centurion called to him, "Come, carry the cross for this man." Protesting and arguing, Simon came forward. The centurion's command rang out louder, "Carry the cross for that man or take the consequences."

Simon didn't recognize Jesus until he was standing beside him. Then with an exclamation of horror, he dropped to his knees and put his arms around the feet of Jesus. "Not you, no, not you, Master," he said, "You healed my boy." Then, springing up suddenly, he ran to the centurion, "I'll carry his cross for him, and if you will let me, I will be crucified in his stead."

This little interlude is not recorded in any of the Gospels, but it is a beautiful illustration of what God's second mile inspires men to do.

12

This Glorious Gospel

I am not ashamed of the gospel of Christ.—
ROMANS 1:16.

For the first twenty years of my ministry I shied away
from this text. It seemed to me to be out of character
with Paul. It was so unlike Paul to be on the *defensive.*
The picture that it painted on my mind was one of Paul
backed up against a wall arguing and justifying his belief
in the gospel, defiantly opposing the people who were
attacking him.

That was not like Paul. Paul was always on the *offensive.*
He was aggressive, driving into new territory with the
banner of his Master unfurled above his head against the
wind. He was eager and earnest for the fray, always moving forward. When they put him out of one city, he went
to another. When he was called on to defend himself be-

fore the Roman governor, he attacked, and the governor trembled. So this negative sentence, "I am not ashamed of the gospel," seemed out of character.

Then one day I found an old Bible with a marginal reading. It read like this: "I am proud of the gospel of Christ for it is the power of God unto salvation." I sprang up from my chair! That was what Paul meant, of course! There was nothing wrong with the text, it was wrong with me. I hadn't read it right. "I'm *proud* of the gospel of Christ." That sounded like him. That's what he meant.

He wrote down here only one reason: "For it is the power of God unto salvation." That, of course, was the prime reason. No one who ever lived would know better than Paul about the power of God and the salvation that the gospel presents. He had experienced it in his own life. He had seen it in the lives of thousands; lives that were transformed, made over, saved from every sin and transgression. This is enough to explain all the sacrifices and sufferings which he endured. But this was only one of the reasons for his being so proud of this glorious gospel, as he called it. He gives four others that round out this picture of the gospel that Paul carried across his part of the world and of which he was so proud.

First, I'm proud of the gospel of Christ, as Paul was, because it picks up our lives and throws them against the background of eternity. This was Paul's thought when he said, "The time for my departure is at hand." By the word "departure" he was indicating that he was not coming to the end of anything, but was just taking a journey. He was almost quoting David's beautiful psalm, "Though I walk *through* the valley of the shadow of death," not *into,* but *through.* One end of it opens wide into this world; the other slants upward to God.

Let me say it this way. Two men were looking at one of the beautiful oil paintings of the famous Turner. It was one of his sunsets. One of the men said to the other, "Aren't the colors too brilliant? Don't they scintillate too much? Aren't they too bright?"

The other, after a little meditation and thought answered: "No, I don't think so. I think that the reason you feel that way about it is because it is framed and hung against a drab wall. God's sunsets are not like that. God's sunsets are splashed against an evening sky. They shade off into the deep purple of the mountains, and up into the blue dome of heaven. There's no frame on either side of them. They just fade out into the north and south."

And I thought how true that is of the gospel of Jesus Christ. It picks our lives up and splashes them against the background of eternity. Life is not framed and hung against drab walls. Life is lived in the power of the gospel of Jesus Christ, saved from all the things from which the gospel saves us. It isn't framed at the beginning by birth or at the end by death. It isn't fenced in. "Ye shall know the truth, and the truth shall make you free," and all the wide world's your range. There are no drab walls against which life is hung. Eternity is out yonder on the other side. There are no blind alleys in God's scheme of things. Death isn't the end of life at all—not when you've read the story of the resurrection of Jesus, the gospel of Jesus that is the power of God unto salvation.

Rather, it's like Ben Bronner, the great old commission merchant said, when I went over to his home at midnight after his wife had called to say, "Ben says he is going home before the day is over." He'd been in a wheel chair for a couple of years, and hadn't been able to lie down at all. When I came in he was asleep, and his wife and two daughters were weeping silently. I sat down close to him and waited, and when he opened his eyes a smile came over his face: "Roy, good news. I've got my long distance call. I'm going home before the day is over, and I'm so glad. Tell my family not to weep. I'm sorry to leave them, but I'm so tired of suffering.

"And Roy, I want you to have some of my things that you and I have enjoyed together through the years." He turned to his wife: "Bring all of my fishing tackle." She piled it up in front of him. "Now, Roy, don't take it and put it away, and show it to people and tell them, 'This was Ben Bronner's,' but take it down to Chesapeake Bay, down to Bloody Point Light, where we have caught so many big ones, and wear it out. I'll be watching you from somewhere and wishing you luck." And after a moment he asked, "Didn't your father die recently?"

"Yes, sir. In December."

"Was he a Christian?"

When I answered, "He was one of the best," he startled me with his next question.

"Don't you want to send him a message? I think I'll know him when I see him over there."

And I did.

"Take my body down to the old burying ground in

Virginia, the old home burial ground, and bury it," he said, "and tell the folks Ben Bronner was smiling when he went home."

I'm proud of the gospel of Jesus Christ that picks up my life and throws it against the background of eternity. Death holds no sting, no fears or hurts. And "ashes to ashes and dust to dust" were not spoken of the soul. I'm proud of the gospel of Jesus Christ.

Second, I'm proud of the gospel of Jesus Christ because it puts the emphasis on the *inside* of man. You remember Christ said, "You keep the outside of the platter clean, but the *inside* of it—you Pharisees, you hypocrites, you whited sepulchres, you are whitewashed on the outside, but the inside is the important part." And the Old Testament reminds us of man: "As he thinketh in his heart, so is he." "Out of it [the heart] are the issues of life."

Someday we'll understand that the most important things are not the visible but the invisible things. Not the tangible and the touchable things of life, but those that we cannot handle with our hands and cannot see with our eyes. There is nothing more real than love and hatred, jealousy and envy, fear and courage—these invisible things, these inside things of life. There is nothing more important than the thoughts that we think, than the meditations of our heart, than the things that we allow our minds to dwell upon and fondle. We *become* those things. They drop down into the bin of our subconscious mind, and by-and-by all of our automatic and reflex actions come from *them*. Not from our planned actions and words, but involuntarily out of this thing that Jesus

110

called our hearts, come the issues of life, the determining factors of life.

Nor is it only true of us as individuals; it is true of us collectively. It's just as true of nations, and it would be well for us to think about our own for a moment—for this gospel of Jesus Christ has a message for *it*.

Macaulay, the great historian of the nations, didn't like Thomas Jefferson, his policies, his plans, or his ideals. So he wrote about the United States of America something like this: "It cannot possibly last, this United States of America. Some strong nation will overrun it from without, or it will be overrun from within. If I turned prophet for once I would say that any nation that ever attacks the United States of America from without will get whipped. I've an idea that they will have such a unity of spirit when it comes to fighting an external foe that nobody could ever conquer them. But this does not mean they will last. It only defers the fall. The fall will come from within. Groups of people with avarice, selfishness, greed for money, position and influence, jealousies from within will undermine it."

Now, Macaulay didn't know anything about "agriculture blocs" and "labor blocs" and power politics and the ideology of communism. He had never seen these things, but he knew the deadly poison of selfishness and greed and avarice and envy, the cardinal sins that grow so naturally in the hearts of men. Here, my brethren, are the *real enemies* of America. And the defense? The gospel of Jesus, the power of God unto salvation—"the blood of Jesus Christ his Son cleanseth us from *all* sin."

Listen to Eric Johnson, past president of the Chamber of Commerce of the United States of America: "When the last war was over, America sat on top of the world with all the gold and the prestige and the power and position and influence, but America was unhappy about the kind of a world in which we lived, and so we said to one another, 'We'll change it. Money can do almost anything. We'll change it. We'll work out a Marshall Plan, and we'll buy the good will of the rest of the world.'

"Oh, we didn't say it quite that bluntly, but that's what we meant. And we started out to set this world up like we thought it ought to be. On the other side of the world there was another nation, Russia, who wanted to change the world, too. They did not like it as it was. They wanted to change it, and rule it themselves, but they did not have the wealth or the gold; so they sent out their emissaries with one word, the word 'Comrade'— 'brother,' in our language—and on the lips of every one of them it was a lie. But even with the lies, that word 'brother' and a smile and an outstretched hand accomplished more than America with her gifts of gold."

Then Eric Johnson stopped and looked at the five or six hundred men before him and repeated quietly this sentence: "Gentlemen, there are some things that money cannot buy. There are some things that money cannot buy. The brotherhood of man is one of them."

Jesus Christ came to earth to organize a brotherhood of man. I'm proud of the gospel of Jesus Christ because it would create a brotherhood built on what's inside of you, friendship, love, neighborliness, and the wish to be

112

of service and help to the rest of the world and to humanity. Jesus put it succinctly when he said, "Thou shalt love the Lord thy God with all thy heart, and with all thy soul, and with all thy strength, and with all thy mind; and thy neighbour as thyself." When we open these hearts of ours to God and love him with all our minds and souls and with all our strength, it's a dangerous thing if we do not find an outlet; *it's dangerous not to love our neighbors,* and turn this power of God into a great brotherhood of man.

Third, I'm proud of the gospel of Jesus Christ because it challenges me to live on the highest level of life, the spiritual level. Not the level of the law, but the level of grace. In an old, old book I found a beautiful illustration of this. A man was talking about these three levels of life, the level of instinct, the level of the law, and the level of the spirit. He said: "I had two dogs. One of them was a tiny Pekinese, and the other a big English bull. One day I turned them loose together in the yard and fed them. Quickly the big bull dog ate his meal, and then he looked over at the plate that belonged to the Pekinese. He walked over and, without even growling, with just the swing of his big head, he knocked the little Pekinese winding and gulped down all of his food."

He continued: "Well, that's the level of the instinct. Take what you can; keep it as long as you can. Push other people out of the way; run over them if necessary. You'll find *that* all through life—the low level of the instinct."

"But I knew," he said, "I must do something about this. So I brought some more food for the little Pekinese, and

113

this time I brought my whip, and when the big bull dog started over toward the little Pekinese, I whipped him soundly. Ever after that when I fed them the bull dog would walk round and round the little Pekinese, drooling and moaning, but he never touched his food. That's the level of the law—when we refrain from doing things because we are afraid of the penalty that is attached."

The writer continued, "There is a higher level. Paul called it the 'level of grace.' We're not under the law, but under grace." Man should live on that level of grace where he doesn't refrain from doing because there is a penalty attached, but because he doesn't *want* to take what belongs to someone else. Man should live where he wants to help others and the direction of his life is giving, not taking—where he wants to be the servant, where he's learned the grand and beautiful lesson of grace. This is the challenge of the gospel of which Paul was so proud.

Finally, I'm proud of the gospel of Jesus Christ because I know God never intended that I should be able to live this life as I want to live it, without the help that Christ can give. The gospel of Christ isn't just the gospel that blazes the way and hangs a signpost up and says: "This is the way. Walk ye in it. This is the road." The gospel of Christ is the power of God unto salvation, and it not only shows me the way, but it gives me the strength and the power and the grace to walk that way and live that way.

With this story I conclude. Down in the heart of Africa a missionary found a little black boy that was much brighter than the rest in his mission class. One day, when the missionary had taught him about all he could, he asked, "Son, how would you like to go to America, to my college, and then come back and be a preacher to your people?"

The little black boy's eyes and mouth popped wide open and he stammered his answer, "O master, if I could. O master, if I could."

The day came when a college professor walked with the little black boy onto the campus. He'd met him down at the train. Suddenly the boy dropped both of his bags. "Professor, look, look! Is that the track team? Is that the cinder track that my missionary told me about? Those boys out there in their white shorts?"

"Yes, that's the track team. They're training," was the answer.

"Well, do you reckon—I know I'm black and they're white, will they let me run with them?"

The professor answered, "I'm pretty sure they will, if you can run. Can you run?"

"Mister, where I come from you have to run to keep alive. Yes, sir, I can run."

The day came when the coach said to the little black boy: "Stay out here. I'm going to let the others go to the showers. I want to clock you on that mile. You've been running away from the others." The coach let him rest a while and then told him, "Toe your mark, get set, go." He pressed down on the stop watch. The black boy's clean, straight limbs just ate up that cinder track. He came sprinting down the home stretch, and as he crossed the line, the coach pressed his stop watch and looked at it. Then he blinked his eyes, shut them, opened them, and looked at it again.

With his mouth hanging a little bit open he said: "Son, this watch must be broken or wrong or something. If it isn't, you have broken the state track record and you've broken it by a wide margin. Son, lie down over there and rest a while and then run it again, will you?" So the little black boy lay down and rested a little, and got up, toed the mark, and away he went again—and the coach watched that stop watch all the way around this time. When he pressed it down again, it was right where it was before within a second.

"Son, you've beaten the state record twice this afternoon. He stood silent for a full minute, and then half aloud he said: "I've got a good pole-vaulter, I've got a good broad-jumper, I've got a good hundred-yard man, this boy can run the half-mile and the mile. I'm going to take a team down to the state track meet. I haven't been down in six years." So they went, a crack team. Just a little team, but they were choice.

When they came to the last event, the mile, the coach gathered his team around him and told them excitedly, "If we win first place in the mile, we'll win the meet by half a point!" To the little black boy he said: "Son, just run like you've been running on our campus. Don't try to run any faster, just run. Get on the outside. Give them a pole. You can run circles around them even on the outside, there won't be anybody in your way."

So the order came, "Toe your mark, get set," the pistol cracked and they were off. The little black boy lagged, all the way around that first lap he was falling farther behind, and the tears were streaming down his face. It looked as if his feet were so heavy he couldn't get them off the ground—as if they were just stuck. Then in the second lap he suddenly exploded into action, caught that group just ahead, and then the next, and the next, and the next, and when they came into the home stretch, he was shoulder to shoulder and chest to chest with the lead man, and then he forged ahead and the tape broke across his chest. He dropped down on the grass panting, and the coach and the team pummeled him and cried and laughed and hugged him, and finally the coach asked, "Son, when you get your breath, tell me what happened."

The little black boy said between panting and gasping for breath, "Coach, my feet were so heavy—I—I couldn't get them off the ground—they—they—they stuck to the ground."

The coach said, "Well, we could see that, but what happened in that second lap?"

"Coach, I prayed."

And the coach said, "You didn't have anything on us. We all prayed." And the coach asked, "Son, what did you say? What was your prayer?"

"Coach, I just said, 'Lord Jesus, if you'll pick 'em up, I'll put 'em down.' And the Lord Jesus pick 'em up so fast I could hardly touch the ground."

Beloved, I'm proud of the gospel of Jesus Christ in the hours of crisis, in the hours of emergency, in the hours when we need some extra help—Jesus is the power of God.

117